8-7-72

PUBLIC PARKS
ON PRIVATE LAND
IN ENGLAND
AND WALES

PUBLIC PARKS ON PRIVATE LAND IN ENGLAND AND WALES

WARREN A. JOHNSON

THE JOHNS HOPKINS PRESS, Baltimore and London

Manufactured in the United States of America
The Johns Hopkins Press, Baltimore, Maryland   21218
The Johns Hopkins Press Ltd., London

Library of Congress Catalog Card Number 73-133554
ISBN 0-8018-1244-5

1703914

CONTENTS

TABLES

FIGURES

ILLUSTRATIONS

Foreword

Americans who have visited England will recognize that the English view of environment and amenity is more sophisticated and
comprehensive than our own. Readers of this work—lawyers, planners, policy makers, private citizens, and students—will find that
this concept can provide us with a badly needed positive perspec-
tive. And since it appears possible that amenity can be both highly
regarded and legally supported in this country, if only because we
are increasingly aware of its lack, Warren Johnson's study of public use of private land is more relevant to the United States than
one might have thought possible even a year ago. As we in the
United States demand more from our surroundings and learn
more about the biological and psychological needs for amenity,
the desire to emulate English practices may increase.

It was a rare pleasure for me to review Mr. Johnson's original
manuscript, since it was so eminently readable, informative, and
entertaining, progressing from the historical and general to specific
analysis and case studies. I was encouraged that, while the author
noted honestly the many differences between English and American
attitudes, traditions, laws and institutions, the similarities were
many and important to consider.

The reader familiar with U.S. environmental programs may
make his own comparisons between English law and administrative
agencies and our own recent National Environmental Policy Act
and our Council on Environmental Quality; he may note the common problems and mandates of national regulatory agencies, and
the common need for access to public lands or waters. He will

recognize, too, that the proclivity of some to build and to love dams is ubiquitous. Most important, he will learn that since man's environmental problems and constraints are similar in different countries, we here should be increasingly critical of our own proposed solutions to these problems.

Mr. Johnson raises some of these problems, and after his extensive study of one English "national park" (a term with a quite different meaning from our own similar term), he discusses how we have handled such problems here. Pointing out the constitutional constraints against the kind of land-use controls described in England, he notes that the law here is in a state of flux. While state and local governments do have the burden of land-use planning, far more federal control over private land use is likely in the future. Likewise, new constitutional doctrines and interpretations, rather than new amendments, promise to be the avenue for real environmental reform in this country. Considering the remarkable growth of private environmental litigation in behalf of public values and the significant court victories in the past few years, there is room for optimism. That we are still saddled with recalcitrant courts and nineteenth-century property attitudes, impossible in a crowded, polluted world, is a challenge to us all.

But already our concern for this new ecological reality has begun to force changes in attitudes toward "life, liberty, and property." We are on our way toward developing more limited concepts of private property and expanded ideas of public property, and if in turn our conception of life and liberty were to include the right to certain environmental amenities, basic land-use regulations could be free of present troublesome constitutional restraints. It will be a difficult process, admittedly, before such development comes about; yet it is helpful to realize that we are not without examples in England of what can be our goal.

MALCOLM F. BALDWIN
Senior Legal Associate
The Conservation Foundation

Acknowledgments

It is largely through the assistance and encouragement of Dr. Charles F. Cooper, Associate Professor of Resource Ecology at the University of Michigan, that this study was written and published. I am happy to be able to acknowledge his special contribution.

While in England I was generously aided by many people. The cooperation of members and staff of the Peak Park Planning Board was especially important, particularly Theo. S. Burrell, Frank F. Forrest and Geoffry Allsop. Others that were helpful were John Foster, Director of the Countryside Commission of Scotland, Professor Denman and Miss Judy Brown of the Department of Land Economy at Cambridge University, and members of the Institute of Agricultural Economics Research at Oxford University and the Countryside Commission in London.

Because the legal aspects of controlling the use of land are so important I especially appreciated the advice of Malcolm F. Baldwin, Senior Legal Associate of the Conservation Foundation, and Joseph L. Sax and Roger A. Cunningham of the University of Michigan Law School.

And finally, I would like to thank my wife, Martha, for her continuous help and encouragement.

Introduction

The English protect and develop the amenities of their countryside for public enjoyment; in the United States we purchase, develop, and operate recreation areas. The difference is quite fundamental, and results in very different leisure resources available to the public in the two countries.

In England virtually all land remains in private ownership but is controlled by public authorities in ways that contribute to its amenity values; but intensive recreation developments in rural areas are rare. In the United States, in contrast, large sums of money are spent on recreation areas but the vast percentage of land receives little public control of land use. The term "recreation," in fact, was rarely used in England until recently, and even now it is most commonly used by those who have had contact with the word in its American context. The English term "amenity," in contrast, is used in a multitude of ways. Like "recreation," it suffers from definitional difficulties, but the rare definition that is found usually indicates a more extensive concept than "recreation."

> . . . amenity is not a single quality, it is a whole catalogue of values. It includes the beauty that an artist sees and an architect designs for; it is the pleasant and familiar scene that history has evolved; in certain circumstances it is even utility—the right thing in the right place—shelter, warmth, light, clean air, domestic service . . . and comfort stations. (Sir William Holford, as quoted in Cullingworth, 1967, p. 133)

Amenity is thus a quality organic to the whole fabric of the environment, and found to a greater or lesser extent in all places. In contrast, recreation is usually defined as an activity, often carried out in a recreation "area," a piece of land set aside and developed for this purpose which is qualitatively different from other lands. Recreation is just becoming important in England and Wales now, as certain parts of the countryside are unable to absorb the numbers of people wishing to enjoy them. This has necessitated the provision of supplementary "country parks," as provided in the Countryside Act of 1968.

Because amenity is so broadly defined and is so fundamental to the way that the English look at their countryside, the provisions for amenity have taken many paths in England and Wales. It is a complicated endeavor, involving continuing interaction between public, semi-public and private bodies. A number of organizations in England, such as the National Trust, the Countryside Commission, and the Nature Conservancy, are without close counterparts in the United States. In addition, there are the traditional English rights to the use of common lands and footpaths. But fundamental to all British efforts are the exceptionally strong planning and land-use control powers provided under the several Town and Country Planning Acts. This is undoubtedly the key to what the English have been able to do in conserving the countryside.

This study will focus on one aspect of this complex situation— albeit a very important one—the public use of private lands for recreational and leisure purposes. To date, the British have not purchased non-urban lands for recreational purposes; Americans find it hard to visualize a national park of hundreds of square miles with virtually no land owned by the national park authorities, but this is what the ten National Parks of England and Wales consist of, and they cover 9 percent of the country. The same is true of the Areas of Outstanding Natural Beauty, which rank just below the national parks in the quality of their landscapes, and comprise 7.3 percent of the land. (See the accompanying figure.)

The Greenbelts surrounding many large urban areas cover 1,094 square miles with an additional 4,473 square miles proposed, for another 9.0 percent. Thus, a total of 25.3 percent of the land of England and Wales has some national designation, or is proposed for designation. The local governments are also permitted to use the designation of Areas of Great Landscape, Historic or Scientific Value in their development plans; and if areas so designated are

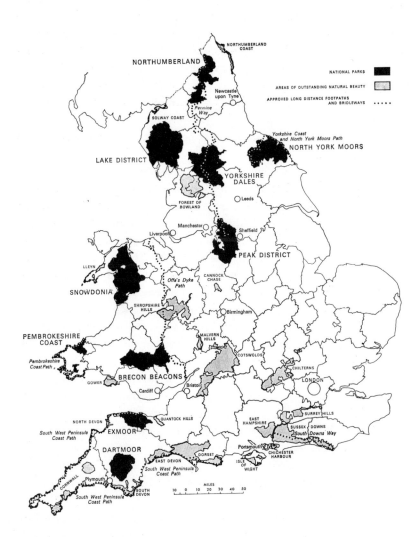

NATIONAL PARKS, AREAS OF OUTSTANDING NATURAL BEAUTY,
AND LONG DISTANCE FOOTPATHS IN ENGLAND AND WALES

added, over 40 percent of the land has some type of amenity designation providing various measures of extra environmental protection (Jellis, 1966). Indeed, the Englishman finds the phrase "public use of private land" confusing. Is not all land private in the sense that someone owns it, whether the government or a private party? The question the Englishman is interested in, instead, regards the rights or privileges granted by the owner to individuals or to the public at large to use the land. Thus, the government gives the public the right to drive on roads, but not to picnic on them.

Part I of this study examines how this very different system has come into being—the influence of geographical factors, the attitudes toward land and its ownership, the background of the planning legislation, its application in rural preservation and the provision of amenity, and how all this combines to provide outlets for leisure pursuits without large-scale governmental expenditures.

Part II is a study of the Peak District National Park. This area was chosen because it is the most aggressively—and by virtually unanimous agreement—the most successfully administered of the national parks. Almost half of the population of England lives within 50 miles of its boundaries (Edwards, 1962, p. 5), including the industrial cities of Birmingham, Manchester, Liverpool, Leeds, and Sheffield. It is also the most accessible national park from the London conurbation. Competition for resources in the park is intense, especially between mineral extraction, water resource development, residential uses, and amenities, although agriculture is the dominant land use. The objective of this study of the Peak District National Park is to analyze how resource decisions which affect the environment are made in this high amenity area, how the English system of land-use control provides an environment with many opportunities for leisure activities without large-scale government expenditures.

Part III, a brief section which follows the main body of this study, evaluates the usefulness in the United States of the English methods of providing leisure opportunities. The evaluation is based on an appraisal of the factors which have remained a part of the common heritage of England and the United States and those which have been lost under the influence of the geography of the American continent and our evolution as a nation.

Throughout this study, only England and Wales will be considered. Scotland and Northern Ireland are administered under different legislations, which although often similar to that in England and Wales, are still separate and are generally studied separately in the United Kingdom. However, to avoid the repetition of "England and Wales" both will be indicated when "England" is used, unless specifically noted otherwise.

part I

The Evolution of the English Methods of Providing Leisure Use of the Countryside

The area of England and Wales is 58,018 square miles, virtually the same as the state of Michigan. The population of England in 1968, however, was 45.8 million, plus 2.7 million for Wales, the total being almost six times greater than the population of the state of Michigan. England's population density in 1968 was 910 persons per square mile; only in 1965 did the population density of our most densely populated state, New Jersey, surpass England's. By the year 2000 England's population is expected to increase 33 percent, to 64.8 million. (Registrar General, 1968:8).

A large population creates environmental pressures and a rising standard of living intensifies them. Many of England's cities contain vast areas of sub-standard, high density dwellings. If these were replaced by houses of the standard of the New Towns, with a density of 10 to 12 houses per acre (which is high by U.S. standards), over two million acres would be needed, 6 percent of the land area of England (Stamp, 1964:252). Since England already imports half of her food, every decrease in the land devoted to agriculture increases this deficit, which must be overcome by the increased export of manufactured goods, a task that is becoming more difficult. The growth of the number of cars is another problem which is already severe, both in the cities and the countryside. Between 1950 and 1965 there was a 400 percent increase in the number of cars, to 9.5 million, and this growth is expected to continue to 25 million in 1985 and to 40 million in 2010 (Central Office of Information, 1968:348). The environmental consequence of this increase is difficult to visualize in such a small country. Use of electrical power is also growing rapidly, more than doubling in the last ten years. Generating plants and the power grid are becoming familiar sights in the countryside.

Even with these pressures on a small country, however, plus others not mentioned, the countryside of England is still extraordinarily attractive, especially to American visitors. It is diverse, intimate in scale, well husbanded and green. This picture of rural life ranks as one of the major tourist attractions of Europe. Travelers pass frequently from one soil type and land form to another, with the associated changes in vegetation, agricultural activity, and traditional building materials. Crop lands, with hedges and woods, change to open grassland, to moorlands, or to village and city-scapes as you cross England in almost any direction, and no point is as much as 100 miles from the sea. Although much of England's attractiveness is due to its natural features, this cannot account for all the beauty and interest of its countryside. Without the works of man, much of it would be covered with dark forests and marshes. Not only has the land been put to productive uses, but these uses are pleasing to the eye. A major factor in this fortunate outcome has been the course that land tenure has taken in England's history.

1

Land Tenure as a Determinant of Man-Land Relationships

THE MEDIEVAL BASE OF LAND TENURE

William the Conqueror took the ownership of all land under his crown after the Battle of Hastings in 1066, and he established in England the most complete feudal system in Europe. To his barons he allotted great areas of the country in return for services in taking England initially and defending it subsequently. Control of each parish was given to a nobleman or soldier, who was referred to as its lord. The Anglo-Saxon serfs were given the right to work the land in return for rendering services or goods to the lord. But to maintain the functioning of the English population, the Normans incorporated into their feudal system a number of the elements of the Anglo-Saxon society.

The Anglo-Saxons had originally come to England in communal groups, and each group settled in a parish which provided all their needs—arable land, a source of water, and what was called waste land, which provided fuel and grazing for animals. The size of the parishs averaged around four square miles. The Anglo-Saxons also brought a larger, improved plow to England, but the heavy, wet soils of most of the country required large teams of oxen to pull the big plows. In order to maintain these large teams, the open field system of agriculture was developed in which the large, unfenced fields of the parish were cultivated and managed by the community.

This system was continued under the Norman feudal system. A manor court was held once a year, and all those with rights to land in the parish were permitted to attend and participate. The court decided how the land was to be worked the following year, punished those who disobeyed the court's rules, and elected several officials to carry out needed functions. With very limited trade, the lord could accumulate only a very limited amount of wealth, primarily the commodities that the craftsmen of the parish could produce. Roads were only mud tracks, and the purity of metals used for money was constantly being debased, both of which discouraged trade. Because the lord often could not utilize the agricultural surplus that accrued to him, the customs of providing feasts and festivals developed, usually in conjunction with the church. Under the feudal system, the laborer lived a lowly life, but he was protected, to a degree, by the system, which was symbolized by the lord, who was responsible for the well-being of his subjects and the productivity of the land on which they all depended. These factors, plus the communal basis of the Anglo-Saxon social organization, brought a type of security to the peasants which differed greatly from the precarious positions they later found themselves in after the feudal system broke down, when poverty, the workhouse, and even starvation were to be feared. However, even after the market economy replaced the feudal economy, the landowners maintained some of the attitudes of the feudal lord when dealing with his tenants.

A characteristic of the medieval era was its stability. Many of the institutions and attitudes which it fostered survive to form the basis of modern land use. The royal forests established by the Norman kings are the forerunners of the English national parks. The common laws pertaining to common land and public right of ways which were established under the feudal system are now keys to the public use of the countryside. And the great estates, which took the place of the feudal lord's manor house, were developed into some of the most famous private landscapes and pleasuring grounds in England, many of which are now open to the public.

THE ROYAL FORESTS

The Normans had a great interest in hunting and sport, and established hunting reserves, known as forests, over a large area of England, up to one-third of all the land according to some estimates (Tansley, 1965, p. 34). In general, these forests were areas of poor quality land which had remained partly uncultivated before the Norman conquest. These wooded, scrubby wastes and moorlands were, however, the best wildlife habitat still remaining. The rights of the farmers who lived in the forests were maintained, but they were subjected to the harsh and much hated forest laws, which forced them to protect the king's wildlife and its habitat. Punishment for killing a wild animal could be death or the cutting off of an arm or hand. Severe laws such as this contributed to the uprisings against the king and the signing of the Magna Carta in 1215, which limited the king's powers. But many woodlands and natural areas were preserved until today because of the forest laws.

The royal forests that were mainly rough open land have come through the ages intact, and a number of them form the heart of the national parks—Dartmoor Forest, Exmoor Forest, the High Peak Forest, and Amounderness and Lonsdale Forests in the Lake District. The only one that is still functioning as a royal forest is the New Forest near Southampton on the south coast, which was established in 1079. Smaller than it was originally, it still covers 145 square miles. The crown has long since changed its activities from hunting to forestry, but common rights remain over much of the forest. The ancient Court of Verderers regulates the ponies that are grazed by commoners, and, since the crown still owns the land, it permits the public to use it for camping, walking, and other activities appropriate to a semi-natural area. The New Forest is managed for the crown by the Forestry Commission primarily for amenity purposes, making special effort to preserve the several ancient woods in the forest. The New Forest is heavily used, and the problems associated with this use have been the subject of several studies (Buchanan, 1966; Forestry Commission, 1968; and New Forest Committee, 1944).

COMMON LANDS AND THE ENCLOSURE MOVEMENT

In the open field system of agriculture, common rights were held to the open fields and the waste, categories into which most of the land of a parish fell. However, these were not common property resources which anyone could use; they were highly restricted and regulated so that they could provide for the needs of the parish. As the population of the parish grew, control became tighter in order to avoid over-use of the land and the damaging of the soil's fertility. As long as the feudal system functioned, this control was effective.

Enclosure was the step that marked the transition from the feudal to the modern, from a contract economy based on the common use of land to a market economy based on private land, cash crops, and trade. Enclosure was the process whereby the common lands were divided into separate parcels of land and distributed to those who owned the land or rights to its use. It is generally considered to have been a necessary step to increase agricultural productivity, since under the communal open field system of agriculture the conservative commoners, fearful of losing their rights, had prevented the adoption of new techniques and the improved breeding of animals. But the process of change itself caused tremendous suffering among those without rights to land, and this is a significant factor behind the still present desire to own land.

As trade developed in the thirteenth and fourteenth centuries, English wool, which was the finest available, became a valuable export. Feudal lords could obtain large financial gains if they could enclose the common lands, turn the open fields and waste into pasture and run sheep on them. Although the king and Parliament controlled the process, the lords generally had a great advantage. For a commoner to obtain his small piece of land, he had to pay his share of the costs of enclosure, which included legal fees plus the cost of dividing the land, building walls or hedges, and sometimes constructing drainage works. Without the necessary capital, many were forced to sell to the lord. Those without common rights received nothing and were turned away from the only places most of them had ever known. Whole villages were razed to the ground. Hundreds of lost villages have been identified by aerial photography (Tate, 1967).

Thus began the pauperism, the begging, and the stealing of the landless who could not find laboring jobs. It was said that the land was raising sheep instead of men. The majority of enclosures were between 1760 and 1820, but the process began in the thirteenth century and continued sporadically for centuries, fluctuating with Parliamentary favor and the price of wool. The people who were turned off the land between 1760 and 1820 provided a ready source of labor for the nascent industrial revolution, which transformed England from a rural country into an industrial nation, a process vividly described by Karl Polanyi in *The Great Transformation* (1944). But this transformation was not completed without a great deal of unrest and peasant revolt, including that of the Levellers, who cut down the hedges and filled the ditches which marked the boundaries of the new fields, and the Diggers, who invaded enclosed land and planted vegetables.

The attractive English countryside that travellers see today is largely the product of the enclosure movement, the small fields bounded by hedges, with frequent hedgerow trees and wildflowers, all of which provides good habitat for wildlife. Today, only 4 percent of the land is subject to common rights, and much of it has management problems from lack of control. The Common Lands Registration Act of 1965 is the first step of a process to put the common lands to productive uses, and recreation is high on the list of proposed uses.

Public Right Of Ways

From Anglo-Saxon times systems of public right of ways have developed across the countryside in response to local needs. A few were planned but most evolved as simple routes to accommodate movements from farm or cottage to village, church, or mill. Later, as the fields were enclosed, right of ways were provided for farmers whose fields were away from existing roads or paths to gain access to their fields by certain specified routes. Some right of ways have grown in use until they are now roads, while many remain as footpaths, and some have ceased to be used altogether.

At first, common law required that a route had to have been used by the public since time immemorial to be a right of way. Later, continuous use within the memory of the oldest inhabitant of the area became adequate, until 1932, when the Rights of Way Act provided that any land actually used by the Public for 20 years without interruption by the landowner was deemed to have been dedicated to the public. Once a right of way is established in this manner, by implied dedication, it cannot be extinguished by non-use (Garner, 1965, p. 68).

In modern times, however, establishment of right of ways by implied dedication is rare, and statutory authority is almost the only way that new footpath right of ways can be created. Numerous pieces of legislation have provided this power, including the Town and County Planning Acts and the National Parks and Access to the Countryside Act of 1949. These powers have not been used extensively, however, because the existing network of footpaths is so vast. Most activity has been involved with relocating and consolidating the existing system to make it more useful for contemporary uses. The national park legislation required all counties to prepare definitive maps of existing footpath right of ways to be used as a basis for improving the system.

Footpaths are of great importance to the public use of the countryside, but there are a number of problems associated with them. Public rights are limited specifically to passage from one point to another over a prescribed route. Picnicking and camping beside the right of way is theoretically illegal, and both depend on the goodwill of the landowner. Trespassing is very common, whether intential or not, because the right of ways cross open pasture or crop land which often have no physical evidence on the ground of where the right of way is; a map is an essential for the walker, unless he is familiar with the route. The footpaths were not established for amenity purposes, and usually pass straight from one point to another instead of following a stream, staying on a ridge top or going to attractive spots. But the major problem stems from the thoughtlessness of ill-informed visitors and vandals who litter the paths, leave gates open, bother the farmer's animals, or tramp on his crops. Local footpath societies try to mend relations with the farmers and provide a certain amount of maintenance. The highway authorities, who are responsible for all right of ways, do very little maintenance on the footpaths. The whole subject has recently been studied by a government committee to plan for the future of the footpath system (Footpaths Committee, 1968).

THE GREAT ESTATES

The era of the great country landowners was from 1688 to 1870, during which time political and economic power rested almost completely with the landed class and particularly with the titled aristocracy. For the most part, these were vigorous and well-educated men who did not disdain administrative and judicial duties as did the French aristocracy, but fostered instead a sense of duty which is still evident today. On the great estates, their power was complete and they managed their lands and their tenants well, making improvements and instituting the new agricultural technology. Many of the great country houses and parks that are such strong tourist attractions today were built or enlarged during this period. Formal Italian and French gardens were built around the houses at first, but 1720 marked the start of the great English tradition of park design. Hundreds of large parks were laid out by William Kent, Lancelot "Capability" Brown, and Humphrey Repton, creating romantic, naturalistic landscapes often thousands of acres in size. Deer herds were established in the parks to complement the scene and to provide game for the hunt. Great woods were planted and many species of trees were brought from different continents and planted with skill and good taste.

The conditions of the farm tenants and laborers varied greatly. At best it was hard work; its worst was indicated by the fact that revolution was a constant threat, especially around the time of the French Revolution. But the medieval pattern of the lord taking a certain amount of care of his subjects existed also during this era between the landowner and his tenants. Adam Smith suggests in *Wealth of Nations* in 1776 that good relations between landowner and tenant was a characteristic of England:

> There is, I believe, nowhere in Europe, except in England, any instance of the tenant building upon the land to which he has no lease, and trusting that the honour of his landlord would take no advantage of so important an improvement. These laws and customs, so favorable to the yeomanry, have perhaps contributed more to the present grandeur of England, than all their boasted regulations of commerce taken together. (Smith, 1909, p. 86)

Generally, most improvements to the farm were made by the landowner, which relieved the tenant of the need to secure capital for improvements, and thus avoided the age-old difficulties usually associated with debt. Investment by the landowner was carried out so extensively that the existence of a "negative economic rent" has been suggested, whereby landowners invested in improvements to the point where other uses of capital would have brought greater economic returns, but agricultural improvements brought other returns to the landowner, mainly social returns from his associates and his tenants, which were highly valued. (Martin, 1958, p. 143).

After 1870, large quantities of cheap agricultural imports from the United States, Australia, and Argentina threw English agriculture into a long depression that lasted until World War II, and virtually destroyed the power of the great estates. This followed abruptly after the richest years of all for agriculture, between 1850 and 1870, but the laissez faire philosophy of the Victorian age of industry and empire had no place for import restrictions, and large quantities of industrial labor were needed. Many marginal farms were abandoned and arable lands were turned to grass. Agricultural production and income sank. Farm buildings, drainage ditches, and hedges deteriorated. The stately homes became heavy liabilities; many were abandoned or only partly occupied to reduce operating costs or turned to use as schools, hospitals, or sanatoriums. Britain fell from a position of being approximately self-sufficient in food production in 1860 to the point in the 1930s when only 35 percent of its food was produced at home.

The nineteenth century brought very mixed results. It was a time of great expansion economically and politically for England, of great but often painful change. In 1800 the population was 9.2 million and predominantly agricultural; in 1900 the population was 32.5 million, and only 6 percent were engaged in farming. The intellectual activity of the era gravitated to the cities and to the British Empire, and the countryside languished and decayed. It was a self-satisfied age, but one which created a heritage of ugliness in the industrial cities and the surrounding coal, iron, and clay fields. The Victorian style of architecture found its way into the countryside in some areas where industrialists and financiers erected gaudy piles of brick in unsuccessful attempts to assume the position of the old landed class. But, fortunately, where the English cities are largely Victorian, the countryside remains largely pre-Victorian, and much more in harmony with the landscape. The industrial cities of the Midlands and the North now are faced with decay and unemployment as new light industries locate in the less damaged environments of the South of England, where the problem is to control a growth which is too rapid.

2

Town and Country Planning

The large industrial cities that grew rapidly during the industrial revolution were unique in that much of the housing was provided by the mill owners. In an era of child labor and 72-hour work weeks, it is not surprising that the houses that were provided workers were small and had low sanitary standards. But this was also a time of rapidly growing knowledge within the medical and public health professions of the factors which influenced health—water supply, sewerage, waste disposal, and space and fresh air. In 1840 a Royal Commission on the Health of Towns was established; when its reports appeared, acts of Parliament soon followed. Protection of the public health was a new role for government; it included measures to give local authorities very limited powers to control street widths and the heights and layouts of buildings, measures that were to develop into town and country planning in the twentieth century.

For a long time the major interest of planning was in the provision of urban housing, mainly for the working class. The first legislation to extend planning to practically all land was the Town and Country Planning Act of 1932. However, under this act very limited powers were made available to local governments, and the plans which resulted were basically zoning plans which tended to ratify existing trends of development. More restrictive plans would have required compensation which local governments could not afford, or which they were unwilling to pay. Very few plans got beyond the preparation stage, and the half of England which was covered by draft plans had enough land zoned for residential use to accommodate 350 million people (Cullingworth, 1967, p. 20).

The 1932 planning act provided an introduction to two problems which were to plague the development of town and country planning, and for which solutions had to be found before planning could become effective. One was how to control development without the expenditure of huge sums of money for compensation, and the second was how to create a unified and effective administrative framework.

However, before the planning legislation can be understood, it is necessary to understand how local government is organized. England and Wales are divided into counties and county boroughs. There is nothing that is equivalent to the states in the United States. Counties are the large areas that England has traditionally been divided into—the familiar Derbyshire. Oxfordshire, Hampshire, Sussex, and so on, of which there are 56. Out of these counties, however, the cities have been removed. These "holes" in the counties are the county boroughs, such as Derby, Oxford, Southampton and Brighton (of the counties named above). There are 73 of these county boroughs, disregarding London, which is administered under a unique arrangement. In effect, the county boroughs are the urban areas and the counties are the surrounding rural areas, although the counties frequently include fairly large towns.

The county boroughs are called "single tiered" authorities because they carry out all the local government functions in the cities, including planning, without further subdivision. The counties are called "three tiered" because they are divided into districts, and each district is comprised of a number of the age old parishes, which now have very few functions. Most local government functions are performed by the counties and the districts.

Under the 1932 Town and Country Planning Act, the authorities responsible for planning in the counties were the districts, of which there are a great number. In fact, 1,440 planning authorities were created by the 1932 Act, and all plans developed had to be approved by Parliament! It is no wonder that the legislation was ineffective. Most of the districts are quite small and without the resources to establish competent planning offices. The districts were weak also in the sense that they were closely tied to local electorates and hence planning was largely aimed at improving the local economy and tax base.

The compensation problem also appeared clearly in the 1932 Town and Country Planning Act, and attempts to solve it were included in practically every town and country planning act which followed for the next 35 years. Under the 1932 Act, compensation had to be paid for the loss of value of land which resulted from planning restrictions. Compensation had to be based on the most profitable possible use of land, even if such use was unlikely. The development value, once it was extinguished from one site by compensation, could "shift" to an adjacent site, and theoretically could be paid on numerous sites when in fact it could never have been realized on more than one or two sites in the absence of planning restrictions. It is, therefore, not surprising that planning involved very little control; zoning land to its most likely use in order to avoid paying compensation was the general rule.

In the thirties England experienced a building boom, especially in the London conurbation and the southeast, the consequences of which are plainly visible today, so unsuccessful was the planning legislation. Residential growth during this period exhibited a number of the characteristics of the U.S. pattern today. Strip development was common and, with the price of land unusually low because of the agricultural depression, housing densities decreased, with more land per house being used than previously. Attitudes toward planning also were similar to those in the United States today in that there was a growing interest in protecting the environment against undesired changes; but this sentiment was not strong enough to overcome the hold of tradition, especially the right of an owner to do largely what he wanted to do with his own land, with compensation required if this right was radically restricted.

World War II profoundly wrenched England away from traditional positions on a number of issues, including the attitude toward stronger powers for town and country planning. The war generated a critical reappraisal of the inadequacies of the way of life that was being fought for, and a powerful commitment formed to put a number of things straight after the war. The destruction of large areas of England's cities by German bombs presented a ready-made opportunity to rebuild them on proper lines.

There was great optimism about what energy, skill, and intelligence could do when applied to the long-standing issues of town and country planning—town design, housing, roads, transport, and open space. This optimism was increased by the success of wartime efforts to increase agricultural productivity, doubling in a few years the percentage of food that was home produced, from 35 to 70 percent. The whole problem of population shifts to the southeast from the depressed industrial cities of the north had come under study just before the war by the Barlow Commission on the Geographical Distribution of the Industrial Population (1940), and wartime powers made control of industrial location a reality with such success that plans for the application of similar powers in peacetime were enthusiastically made.

Even though later planners looked back wistfully on the nearly forgotten confidence and optimism of the war years and immediately thereafter, there can be no doubt that a fundamental change occurred during these years. The idealism waned after the heavy sacrifices of wartime were no longer necessary, but not before the passage of legislation which was of basic importance to the fine appearance of much of the English countryside. The ground work for this post-war legislation was prepared during the war. In its 1942 report, the Scott Committee on Land Utilization in Rural Areas recommended, among many other things, the establishment of national parks, nature reserves, and other leisure developments. The Uthwait Committee on Compensation and Betterment was also established in the dark days of 1941, and the confidence and enthusiasm that both of these committees attest is in itself amazing. These two reports, together with the report of the Barlow Commission mentioned above, constitute the famous trilogy which so greatly influenced post-war planning legislation.

The legislation was delayed somewhat after the end of the war by the question of whether comprehensive planning powers should be given to a new Ministry of Town and Country Planning, which, it was feared, might dominate the other ministries, or whether the planning powers should be fitted into the existing ministries, with each handling the parts which related to its functions—the Ministry of Health, of Transport, of Labour, and so on. It was feared, of course, that this would hopelessly fragmentize planning. A compromise was worked out which has not been completely satisfactory, for although a separate Ministry of Town and Country Planning was created, its powers, though quite broad, were not as wide as many planners had wished. But a number of powers were left with other ministries, with co-ordination to be achieved through consultation. A subsequent reorganization of the Ministry of Town and Country Planning in 1951 changed its name to the Ministry of Housing and Local Government, which is initially misleading until it is recalled that planning is primarily a local government responsibility. The designation Ministry of Housing and Local Government will be used throughout, even though there have been several changes in Cabinet organization and ministerial responsibilities.

THE 1947 TOWN AND COUNTRY PLANNING ACT

The 1947 Town and Country Planning Act is the landmark piece of legislation which brought virtually all development under planning control. The major tool by which this was accomplished was the requirement that before any development could be undertaken planning permission must be obtained from the planning authorities. The decision of whether or not to grant planning permission was to be based partly on the development plans prepared by each county and county borough, which had replaced the districts as the planning authorities (thus reducing the number of planning authorities from 1,440 to 145). The development plan was not to provide detailed plans or maps, but was to provide general directions only. For instance, the plan would indicate which towns could accept industry, would allocate areas for housing, and would designate areas which were to be left in open space uses. But a developer could not be sure of receiving planning permission even if his proposal conformed to the development plan because the planning authorities were to base their decision on many criteria, some of which could not be covered by the plan. The planning authorities could thus exercise a great deal of discretion in making their decision. Their major restraint, however, was that an unsuccessful applicant for planning permission could appeal to the Minister of Housing and Local Government, who could overrule the decision of the planning authorities after a public hearing. Also, since the Minister was to co-ordinate the plans for

regional and national objectives, the development plans had to
have his approval.

The Compensation Question

Finally, and most radically, the development value of all land
in England was to be nationalized under the provisions of the
1947 Town and Country Planning Act. After nationalization, landowners would own only the rights to land in its 1947 uses; subsequently, the community's interests were to take precedent over
the landowner's. The logic of this was that it was the community
which had created the development values in the first place, and
not the individual. Because of this, the community's interest should
be paramount in deciding the use that was to be made of the
land, and the community should benefit from the development
value it had created. One critic has complained that this is a return to feudal ways, which, roughly taken, is correct (Marlowe, 1965),
in that the individual's interest is subordinate to the community's.

Compensation for the development values which were to be
nationalized was to be paid once and for all from a universal fund
of £300 million ($1.2 billion at the then current exchange rate).
These funds were to be distributed in proportion to the amount of
the development values taken, but the full development value
would not be paid. It would be discounted to avoid compensation
of "shifting" values (see page 13 above). Hence, the £300 million
figure, which was estimated to be the total development value that
existed at the date. After nationalization, owners of land on which
development was permitted were to pay to the government a development charge of 100 percent of the increased value of the land
in its new use; suggestions that the development charge be less than
100 percent were rejected by the Labour Government at this time
when there was a strong move toward nationalization. When planning permission was refused, no compensation was to be paid, in
conformance with the logic of the scheme.

This compensation plan caused so many problems that it jeopardized the whole planning effort in a tumult of political struggle
and administrative tie-ups. Suffice it to say that the scheme was
not carried out. It was a major issue in the 1951 election and in
the victory of the Conservative party, which soon passed the 1953

Town and Country Planning Act, removing the 100 percent development charge completely—going from one extreme to the other. The £300 million fund was only to be used to provide compensation for the loss of development values from planning restrictions which accrued up to the time that the 1947 act went into effect but not for development values which accrued thereafter. This was handy, but there was little logic in it. This decision did, in effect, nationalize the post-1947 development values of land which did not receive planning permission, since such land was to be held in present uses without compensation. Thus, planning permission could make land very valuable while similar land without permission would be worth far less. This frequently happened, especially with respect to agricultural land that had potential for residential development. But although it was quite unequal in its impact, the 1953 act resulted in freeing much land for building. A severe land shortage had developed because landowners had been reluctant to sell land or develop it when they could not realize a gain but had to pay the 100 percent development charge instead. This did not bother the Labour Government too much since it emphasized public housing, but the Conservative Government aimed more at private house construction.

When the Labour party returned to office in 1964 they set about fulfilling a campaign promise by passing the Land Commission Act of 1967. This legislation has gone a long way toward ameliorating the inequalities of the compensation policy. A betterment levy of 40 percent, later to rise to 50 percent, of the development value is to be paid to the Land Commission when realized. This figure was set to encourage development while reducing the disparity between land for which planning permission is given and that for which it is denied. The betterment levies will go into a fund which the Land Commission can use to purchase by compulsion land needed for development, to make sure that "the right land is available at the right time" (Labour Government, 1965, p. 1). In theory at least, this gives the government an opportunity to contribute more positively to planning, and to go beyond the essentially negative powers of denying undesirable developments. Since 1967, planning authorities have been able to contribute to the achievement of desired development by purchasing land and then reselling it with specific building requirements. The additional powers of compulsory purchase were needed to offset the claim of the Conservative party that it would abolish the Land Commission when it returned to power, thus encouraging landowners to hold back land from development. However, it now appears that the Conservatives will only modify the Land Commission Act. If utilized effectively, the Land Commission could play a constructive part in town and country planning.

Thus the compensation question rests for the time being. Such an intensely political matter can never be "solved," but the general feeling seems to be that the real stumbling blocks have been passed and the planning process is beginning to stabilize. The concept of controlling development in conformance with a plan that is enforced by competent planners has not been in the center of the dispute. These powers, which are fundamental to the preservation of the countryside, have been widely accepted as necessary and functional. But until the compensation problems were at least reduced, the existence of the other planning powers were not secure.

The Planning Structure and Machinery

The 1947 Town and Country Planning Act reflects a desire to decentralize as much planning responsibility as possible to the counties and county boroughs while retaining adequate power in the central government to provide for the needs of co-ordination and a measure of supervision over the counties' efforts. Basically, the local planning authorities prepare the plans and carry them out. The Minister of Housing and Local Government approves the plan and adjudicates appeals in cases where a developer has been refused planning permission by planning authorities; in these cases the decision of the Minister is final. Appeals are frequent, numbering 12,000 in 1966, and on the average nine months are required for a decision (Labour Government, 1967, p. 7). The Minister allows between 15 and 20 percent of the appeals that are made to him, and his appeal decisions serve to establish the government's position with regard to the geographical areas concerned. Court appeals against ministerial decisions are rare because they can only be made on questions of law, and not of planning wisdom.

Violations of planning controls established by the planning authorities are handled by the issuance of enforcement notices. If the unauthorized activity does not cease, an enforcement order is issued. An enforcement order can be appealed to the Ministry, which is often done because the violator has nothing to lose; at the same time, he gains about nine months while waiting for the inquiry and the Minister's decision. If the Minister upholds the order and the violation does not cease, the next step is in the local court, where the offender, if found guilty, is fined. Often the fine is initially small, but it can be repeated if the violation continues and may result in a fine being levied every day that the violation continues. However, this process is slow and cumbersome, and many minor violations and some larger ones escape enforcement.

The relationship between the Ministry and the local planning authorities is generally supportive and has been described as a "partnership" where "there is no pressure for a take-over of functions by the Ministry" (Cullingworth, 1967, p. 47). If anything, the Ministry is trying to reduce their involvement, especially in the number of details and appeals, which is the major goal of the 1968 Town and Country Planning Act. The Ministry assists the local planning authorities by providing technical guidance and establishing procedures for carrying out many of the provisions of these complex acts.

Complexity, in fact, is one of the most notable aspects of the town and country planning acts. Part of this stems from the requirement that legislative history cannot be referred to in carrying out legislation in England. Only the words of the act can be utilized in interpreting it; thus legislation is carefully and exhaustively written so that every eventuality is covered. But much of the complexity is also inherent in the planning job itself. There is no written constitution in England, other than the Magna Carta; Parliamentary statutes are controlling. Parliament is thus free to draft wide-ranging and comprehensive legislation without difficult questions of constitutionality. It is because of this that Parliament can pass legislation such as the planning legislation which requires hundreds of pages to cover completely. Even defining just what constitutes development, for example, is a long process. As a result, planners rarely use the acts themselves, but rely on administrative devices, handbooks, and ultimately on the advice of the clerks (lawyers) of the planning authority offices.

Since the 1947 Town and Country Planning Act established a separate planning ministry but did not give it complete planning powers over the other ministries, arrangements had to be provided to obtain the desired co-ordination, both at the cabinet level and at the level of the local planning authorities. To the degree that this is accomplished, it is usually done by various types of required consultation. For instance, the Minister of Housing and Local Government must consult the Minister of Transport before approving the location of trunk roads on development plans. And no application for an industrial building of 5,000 square feet or more can be approved without an Industrial Development Certificate from the Board of Trade. In a number of these situations the powers of the Minister and the local planning authorities are inadequate to accomplish the desired co-ordination of planning. The Forestry Commission can establish new plantations and cut down woods without planning permission, since agriculture and forestry activities are not considered to be development and are exempt from planning control. For the same reason, farm buildings can generally be replaced or new ones built without planning permission. Communication masts have been erected on hilltops, defense maneuvers carried out on wild moorlands and overhead power lines built through attractive sections of the countryside against the wishes of the Ministry or the local planning authorities. For the preservation of the countryside, the Ministry's lack of authority in such cases is the greatest weakness in the planning legislation.

Parliament has supported the preservation of amenities more strongly than the ministries. When local governments seek Parliamentary approval for airports, reservoirs, or other developments in high amenity areas, Parliament has frequently rejected them. However, in part this may be due to the responsibilities of the ministries for finding the land for needed developments. A characteristic problem is that there is no really suitable place for almost any large development, and numerous arguments can be set forth against a particular site which may still be the best site available.

For the most part, the planning structure and machinery has been established very much as it was visualized during the war. The major disappointments have been with the positive powers. The system of requiring planning permission to prohibit undesirable development has been reasonably successful. But positive actions to create a good environment have been limited, especially in the cities where rapid growth and change have created strong pressures. In the countryside, however, the paucity of action of a positive nature is not such a disadvantage since the restriction of development through planning controls is an excellent way to preserve the traditional character of the countryside. Whereas the cities cannot stand still but yet cannot find a way to grow gracefully, the desired appearance of the countryside survives best when change is minimized. Conservative rural interests generally oppose the intrusion of urban type developments (and, it should be added, of urban visitors), and substantial support is received from urban preservation groups, backed up by the English public's widespread sentiment for preservation. Even a powerful and independent government agency like the Central Electricity Generating Board finds it virtually impossible to find sites for generating plants which are free from intense and well-organized local opposition.

The positive provisions for the leisure use of the countryside, however, as with the positive provisions of the town and country legislation, have been less successful. Preservation of the environmental resource is a very important thing, but its further enhancement and the provision of facilities for its enjoyment is also important.

3

Legislation for the Leisure Use of the Countryside

World War II had the same effect on legislation for national parks, nature reserves, and access to open lands that it had on town and country planning. Traditional opposition was swept away in a surge of enthusiasm for making a reality of wartime visions.

There had never been a shortage of ideas and proposals for national park legislation. In fact, England may be able to claim the first clear expression of the national park concept. William Wordsworth greatly loved the Lake District, probably the most famous landscape in England, and in his *Guide to the Lakes*, published in 1810, he included a plea that the Lake District be deemed a "sort of national property, in which every man has a right and interest who has an eye to perceive and a heart to enjoy" (Wordsworth, 1906, p. 92). This statement, besides presenting the idea of a national park, also illustrates well the traditional English attitude toward land tenure. Even though a "national property" is suggested, only a right to use it is spoken for, and then only for those "with an eye to perceive and a heart to hear," since at this time common rights were rarely available to the public at large, but limited to certain individuals or groups. As the spokesman for the romantic reaction to industrialism, Wordsworth had wide influence.

In 1884 the first legislation was introduced in Parliament to permit public access to open lands, the Access to the Mountains Bill, but this bill and numerous subsequent bills were not passed. A weak bill was passed in 1939, but it was never put into operation be-

cause of the war. The major opposition was from the shooting interests who claimed that hikers would be detrimental to the number
of birds that could be raised on the highlands.

As failure to obtain access to private open lands continued, public interest turned toward the establishment of national parks,
stimulated by such parks being established in the United States,
Canada, and Africa. But although a government committee (The
Addison Committee) supported a policy for national parks in
1931, no action was taken. During the war the Scott Committee on Land Utilization in Rural Areas emphatically supported
national parks as long overdue, as well as a number of other
programs for the public use of the countryside, most of which appeared in subsequent legislation. Soon after the Scott report was
completed, two reports on national parks followed in quick
succession, *National Parks in England and Wales*, by John
Dower in 1945, and the *Report of the National Park Committee*,
by the Hobhouse Committee in 1947. The Dower Report was a per-
sonal report to the Minister of Town and Country Planning, stating the general case for national parks. The Hobhouse Committee
report, which followed, was more exhaustive; but both reports agreed
on fundamental issues. A national park was defined as "an extensive area of beautiful and relatively wild country, in which, for
the nation's benefit and by appropriate national decision and
action, a) the characteristic landscape beauty is strictly preserved,
b) access and facilities for public open-air enjoyment are amply
provided, c) wildlife and buildings and places of architectural and
historic interest are suitably protected, while d) established farming
is maintained" (Dower Report, 1945, p. 6). The administrative organization proposed was appropriate to a truly "national" park; it
was to be supported fully by central government funds distributed
through a National Parks Commission. The planning authorities
responsible for each park would be appointed half by the local
governments and half by the Minister of Town and Country Planning, and the Minister would also appoint the chairman. The
Hobhouse Committee believed that about one-tenth of the land
within a national park would be purchased by the government for
public use and preservation purposes, and substantial capital expenditures were proposed (Hobhouse Committee, 1947, p. 68). The
Dower Report suggested 10 areas for national park designation and

the Hobhouse Committee 12, mainly centering on the highland of the western half of the country, and the parks which exist today are quite close to those proposed in the reports. Lands which did not quite meet the standard of a national park were recommended for designation as conservation areas, later termed Areas of Outstanding Natural Beauty.

The National Parks and Access to the Countryside Act, 1949

Although the national park legislation which followed accepted many of the recommendations of the two reports, it did not incorporate several key provisions. Under the act, a National Parks Commission was set up in London under the Minister of Housing and Local Government and was charged with the duty of

> . . . exercising the functions conferred on them by the following provisions of this Act—a) for the preservation and enhancement of natural beauty in England and Wales, and particularly in the areas designated under the Act as National Parks or as Areas of Outstanding Natural Beauty; b) for encouraging the provision or improvement, for persons resorting to National Parks, of facilities for the enjoyment thereof and for the enjoyment of the opportunities for open air recreation and the study of nature afforded thereby . . . . (Section 1, National Parks and Access to the Countryside Act, 1949).

The National Parks

The first job for the commission was to designate the national parks, which was done by order after confirmation by the Minister. Prior to making the order the National Parks Commission had simply to "consult with every . . . county council, county borough council and country district council whose area includes any land in the areas to be designated a Park" (Section 7, National Parks and Access to the Countryside Act, 1949). The characteristic directness of the Parliamentary system is illustrated by the simplicity of this process. In 1951 the Peak District National Park was the first park designated, followed by five others within two years. The tenth and last park was designated in 1957, the Brecon Beacons National Park in Wales. Although there has been some discussion of additional parks, none have received serious consideration.

But the administrative and financial arrangements for the parks were not to embody the "national" concept recommended in the Dower and Hobhouse reports. The act did call for national park authorities to be set up for each park; these authorities would also act as the local planning authorities, but two-thirds of their memberships were to be appointed by the counties and one-third by the Minister of Housing and Local Government. The chairman was to be chosen from within the group, and he is thus usually a county representative.

If a park fell into more than one county, a single planning authority was to be created for the park, and the park lands would be removed from the planning jurisdiction of the county planning authorities. However, the act also permitted, if the Minister so chose, the establishment of a joint advisory board which would simply advise the existing county planning authorities on national park matters, a much less satisfactory arrangement. The first two parks set up by the Labour Government, for the Peak District and the Lake District, had full planning authority, but the Conservative Government which came in later in 1951 was unwilling to continue this policy because of opposition from local governments. Instead, they established four parks with joint advisory boards. The four other national parks were within one county and are under the direction of a committee of the main county planning authority, as provided by the act. Only one park, the Peak District National Park, has its own office and planning staff; all the others rely on the staff of the constituent county planning authorities (Blenkinsop, 1964).

The fear, of course, was that the national parks would be dominated by the local interests and administered for local ends under this arrangement. The financial arrangements tended to confirm this fear. All administrative expenses of the park planning authorities were to be born by the constituent counties. Programs undertaken under the National Park and Access to the Countryside Act to provide for public enjoyment of the parks include provisions for the local planning authorities to receive grants from the central government for 75 percent of the cost. But since even the 25 percent of such costs would be an increase in the already tight budgets of rural counties, very little money has been spent. In addition, since urban visitors are not especially welcome in agricultural areas, the provision of facilities for their benefit is a low priority expenditure for the counties. Important amenity improvements, such as purchasing derelict sites or non-conforming developments, are far beyond the financial resources of most rural counties for even their 25 percent of the cost.

Several reasons have been given as to why the government decided on this arrangement, against the suggestions of its two committees who studied the question and the objections of those who wanted stronger national park legislation. One reason was that the newly constituted planning authorities established by the 1947 Town and Country Planning Act were just getting underway and the government did not want to suggest that they were not capable of carrying out this new responsibility. The government was also reluctant to take away more responsibility from the local governments; this had occurred with a number of other functions in the recent past and each time there was stiff opposition from the well-organized local governments. And perhaps most important, the government may not have been convinced that national parks on more traditional lines would work in a densely populated country, or that local conditions would permit the parks to be implemented aggressively.

Whatever the reason, these administrative and financial arrangements have set the pattern for the operation of the national parks, and in spite of insistent support for stronger measures the basic scheme seems likely to continue. The recent Countryside Act of 1968 was specifically drawn up to bring the 1949 legislation up to date and to provide for new needs, but it made no significant changes in the administration of the national parks. During the 1967–68 fiscal year, the grants to the ten national parks from the central government amounted to only £208,960 for the support of such activities as interpretive and warden (ranger) services, provision of overnight accommodations (under certain conditions only), tree preservation, treatment of derelict land, and access to open lands. Expenditures by local governments totaled £380,195 (National Parks Commission, 1968, p. 54). Many of the local government expenditures are for planning activities required by the town and country planning legislation and would have been incurred even if the national park had not existed, a further indication of how little is spent on the English national parks.

The National Parks Commission

The commission is primarily an advisory body. The matters that it can influence most, such as the designation of national parks, approval of park development plans, and the appointment of members to the park planning boards, are all actually matters over which the Minister of Housing and Local Government has authority. This is in conformance with the general policy that the Minister should have strong central control over all planning. However, the function of the National Parks Commission is expanding and is now not limited to national parks; the commission has become the government's watchdog for amenity matters for the whole country, and this role is reflected in its new (1968) name, the Countryside Commission which will be used hereafter in this book. This involvement stems largely from the amenity clauses which are found in much recent legislation which affects the countryside. This clause first appeared in Scotland's Hydro-Electric Development Act of 1943, which required the authorities "in the exercise of their functions, to have due regard to the desirability of preserving the beauty of the scenery and objects of architectural or historic interest . . ." (Bracey, 1963). Similar clauses were subsequently inserted in legislation for government water resource development in England and for forestry, electrical generation and distribution, and other government enterprises which affect the landscape. The Countryside Commission has performed as consultant for the government in these cases, identifying the amenity issues and suggesting how they could be resolved or, at least, how the impact of unavoidable developments could be softened. Its position within the government puts the commission in a much more favorable position than the private preservation societies to affect these issues. Legislation in the United States frequently includes similar environmental protection clauses but their impact has been limited by the absence of a mechanism for effectuating them; it may be that the recently established Council of Environmental Quality can perform the watchdog role, at least on the activities of the federal government. The Countryside Commission also serves as a clearing house of information and research, as well as providing advice to local governments when requested.

Access to the countryside

The access provisions of the National Parks and Access to the Countryside Act make it legislation that planners all over England are familiar with, even if there are no nationally designated amenity areas nearby. The act required every county to make a survey of footpaths and to show them on a map which could be challenged, after which a definitive map of existing public right of ways would be published. Other parts which pertained to footpaths were later superseded by the encyclopedic Highway Act of 1959.

The Countryside Commission was empowered to designate long-distance routes for hikers by procuring the right of ways and funding their improvement and maintenance. The only long-distance route to be completed so far (1969) is the Pennine Way, starting at the southern end of the Pennine mountains in the Peak District National Park and continuing 250 miles to the Scottish border, although several other routes are well on their way to completion. Because of the full financing of these routes by the central government there has been much activity to develop them, but progress has been slow because of the difficulties of acquiring the right of ways.

Under English law the "right to roam," or the right to move at will over a piece of land without staying on a specified route, is viewed very differently than right of way, in that the public cannot acquire a right to roam through use. The right to roam can only be acquired by the dedication of a specific grant to the public by the landowner, which is rare (Harris, 1965, p. 128). The 1949 act provides a way to obtain public access to open land through the use of access agreements and access orders without a formal, and thus permanent, dedication. If negotiations for an access agreement with a landowner fail, an access order can be made, permitting public access without the owner's consent. Only one access order has been issued; usually the threat of one is enough to encourage an obstinate owner to negotiate. Compensation is payable after five years on the presentation of evidence of damage by the landowner. Access land in national parks and areas of outstanding natural beauty, where most efforts have been focused, amounted to only 61,300 acres in 1968, of which 78 percent is in the Peak District National Park (National Park Commission, 1968, p. 52).

Areas of outstanding natural beauty

These areas, which are designated in the same way as national parks, are administered by the local government planning authorities without special arrangements. The designation serves primarily to encourage a higher standard of environmental protection, and the 75-percent grants (see p. 25) are available for special work on the same basis as for the national parks. New areas of outstanding natural beauty are being designated each year, including a number along the coast, and land so designated may soon surpass that of the national parks.

Nature Conservancy

The National Parks and Access to the Countryside Act also established the Nature Conservancy, whose purpose is to purchase and operate nature reserves. However, since the land is generally purchased or leased by the government, and since the public is generally excluded (both qualifications are becoming harder to make), and since the purpose is scientific study rather than public leisure use, the Nature Conservancy is only peripherally relevant to this study. In 1965 it was incorporated in the Natural Environment Research Council.

THE COUNTRYSIDE ACT, 1968

More than anything else, this act suggests for the first time the appearance of a new trend in legislation for leisure, a trend in the direction of recreation as it is known in the United States. In 1966 a White Paper was issued by the government, *Leisure in the Countryside*, which set out the government's position, and the Countryside Act followed it closely. The White Paper suggested that the rising public use of the finest parts of the countryside was beginning to result in signs of strain, mainly in congestion of the roads and over-use of a number of well-known places:

> The Government accordingly propose . . . what might be called "Country Parks." These would serve three purposes. They would make it easier for town-dwellers to enjoy their leisure in the open, without travelling too far and adding to congestion on the roads; they would ease the pressure on the more remote and solitary places; and they would reduce the risk of damage to the countryside—aesthetic as well as physical— which often comes about when people simply settle down for an hour or a day where it suits them, somewhere "in the country"—to the inconvenience and indeed expense of the countryman who lives and works there (Labour Government, 1966, p. 6).

The Countryside Act leaves the local governments much leeway in deciding what type of parks they wish to provide, but fairly intense recreational use is visualized. The seventy-five-percent grants will be payable for the cost of purchasing land and developing facilities. Country parks can even be established within national parks, which is illustrative of what national parks are not today. However, it is expected—in lieu of trying to overcome local reluctance to support parks for urbanites who come from far away to the better-known areas—that the country parks will be provided primarily by the counties with large urban populations who are willing to support recreation. It was a logical decision and early indications are that the response to the program may be strong.

Additional research by the Countryside Commission was also authorized by the Countryside Act. The main research technique to be utilized is the field testing of experimental schemes to facilitate the enjoyment of the countryside.

In retrospect, the 1949 national park legislation seems to have provided adequate powers to the wrong bodies, to the rural counties who were not interested in providing facilities for the use of city people. The Countryside Act extends similar powers to the right bodies. But since the country parks will provide recreation on government-owned land, they are outside the scope of this study.

4

Other Influences on Public Use of the Countryside

THE PRESERVATION MOVEMENT

Even though Wordsworth, Ruskin, and others provided the basis for a preservation movement early in the nineteenth century, what could be called a movement did not materialize until later in the century. For the most part, threats to the countryside were minor until after the agricultural depression in the 1870s. The railroad and canal networks did spread rapidly, but, as with the automobile later, they were generally felt to be a help in getting to the countryside to enjoy it.

The first clear threats were the efforts to enclose common lands which were used by the public for recreation and amenity purposes, mainly around London. In 1865 the Commons, Open Spaces and Footpath Preservation Society was formed to resist this trend. When protection was achieved, however, these lands often became so popular with the public that the owners were unable to put them to any profitable use. When the owner was the crown, as in the New Forest, the situation was accepted, but where the land was privately owned it soon became necessary to purchase it specifically for public use.

The major threat to the historic values of the countryside was the agricultural depression after 1870 when many historic houses and places formerly occupied and taken care of were abandoned and left to deteriorate. This led to the formation of the National Trust for Places of Historic Interest and Natural Beauty—the National Trust—in 1895, and it is now an important English institution, with other European efforts being patterned after it.

The National Trust accepts for the nation donations of land and historic buildings which it holds as a trustee, protecting them while permitting the public to visit them. The Trust is an independent organization, although the government has given it valuable assistance. In 1907 the National Trust Act allowed the Trust to declare land inalienable; it cannot be acquired by compulsion except with Parliamentary authority. Also, individuals who donate property or funds to the Trust can receive credit for this against their death duties. However, the Trust will accept only properties which have genuine historic or natural values and which also can be made to be self-supporting, which can be difficult for historic buildings. Owners often must contribute money to meet this requirement before the Trust will accept their property, but once it is met the owners can continue to live in the house, providing it is opened to the public on a scheduled, if limited, basis. It is generally considered desirable to have Trust properties lived in, not only to provide upkeep but to present a more attractive and lived in appearance to visitors.

However, balancing these two uses of a property—public viewing versus operating it as a private estate to produce income—has been difficult for the Trust; in many ways, they conflict. The Trust has been criticized for being too preservation-oriented and for not providing sufficient public access to its properties, which now number over 1,000 on more than 400,000 acres of land, including much of England's treasure of historic and natural properties. The Trust maintains that it has received such good public support for high-quality preservation and not for public use. In 1968, its 159,000 members paid membership fees of £239,547, and legacies amounted to £772,238. This enabled the Trust to overcome its operating deficit of £233,000 and to purchase properties of high historic or natural value that come on the market. In contrast, the proceeds from the small admission fees that it charges to its properties are minor. The Trust does not want to jeopardize its support by encouraging heavier use or its independent status by accepting government funds. The critics reply that the Trust has already received huge amounts of public funds through lost death duties and should be more responsible to the public at large (National Trust, 1968; Fedden, 1968).

There are other national organizations, such as the Naturalists Association, the Council for Nature, and the Civic Trust, but the majority of preservation activities are carried on by small, local organizations. There are several reasons for this difference with the United States, where most efforts have been on a national basis. First, the central government in England has not become directly involved in large preservation schemes but has passed legislation which is primarily the responsibility of local authorities to carry out. Thus, it is up to local groups to protect local amenities, especially under the town and country planning acts. Second, regional loyalties remain strong in England. Regional differences are great and have been maintained by groups organized on the basis of a county, an area of outstanding natural beauty, or a town. And finally, a number of groups have been formed to preserve all sorts of different features, from windmills to odd architectual details.

But there was a need for a strong, unified voice to speak for the preservation interests on national issues, so in 1926 the preservation organizations got together and established the Council for the Preservation of Rural England (C.P.R.E.). Its role is to be the spokesman for the movement as a whole, to keep a close eye on the ministries and Parliament, and to co-ordinate the efforts of the many preservation organizations. By general consent, it has been very effective. The preservation movement has maintained its unity far more successfully than in the United States, where the tendency is for different groups to split off to express different points of view. Again, this is probably due to the vast range of decisions made in Washington or by the federal government in general. Specialization of interest on the part of preservationists, as seen in the United States, would not be so likely if they were involved primarily with county or village issues!

There are also a number of groups which represent various recreational activities, such as camping, caravaning (trailers), mountaineering, youth hosteling, field sports, and others. One of the largest is the Ramblers' Association, which has actively worked for improvements in footpaths, long distance routes, and access agreements. In the thirties when landowners of the high moorlands of the Peak District would not permit hikers on their land and

pressed trespass charges, the Ramblers organized a mass trespass
to publicize their aims.

THE INTEREST OF LANDOWNERS

For problems like this, the landowners turn to the Country Landowners Association. Anyone owning land can join this group, although the term "country landowner" usually suggests a holder of a
large estate. The official policies of this group are actually quite
moderate, centering on holding the best agricultural land in that
use. It accepts that public use of the countryside is going to grow,
and it has strongly supported the idea of country parks. A number
of landowners, in fact, have a stake in public use in that the proceeds from opening their homes and parks to the public are an important source of income to them. In 1966, 599 stately homes
were open, several of which actively promoted visitation by providing museums, zoos, jazz festivals, and other attractions. Such
operations are the subject of a book by a successful landowner,
Lord Montague, under the title *The Gilt and the Gingerbread,
Or How to Live in a Stately Home and Make Money* (1967).

The National Farmers' Union (N.F.U.) is a huge organization
which represents the farmer's interest on all issues, and thus forms
the core of the opposition to measures which would tend to increase public use of rural areas. The N.F.U. is an extremely
powerful organization, mainly through its close ties with the Ministry of Agriculture and its formal role in setting prices under the
agricultural assistance program. The high level of this assistance,
however, is a major factor in the preservation of the rural landscape. Without it, there would be a great deal of rural poverty,
and many marginal farms would cease production and become
derelict. This positive force may be as important to the preservation of the countryside as the town and country planning acts,
perhaps more important because of the negative nature of the
planning powers. The agricultural supports also help to keep the
price of agricultural land up, discouraging non-agricultural uses.
Agricultural land prices are now four times greater than they were
10 years ago and average £243 per acre in 1967 (*Country Landowner*, April 1968, p. 101).

Agricultural assistance is a double-edged sword, however, when grants are paid for replacing farm buildings several hundred years old with large metal buildings or to plow up and enclose open land. One respected analyst has predicted that the countryside as it appears today is soon to be replaced by a streamlined industrial plant (Weller, 1968).

Agriculture is the most protected industry in England; it is the only domestic industry for which protection is asked in England's application to the European Common Market. There is very little public feeling for reducing the costly support program; if anything there is interest in increasing agricultural output to reduce imports of agricultural products, which must be paid for by exports. However, the decreasing marginal returns from further investment in intensifying agricultural production make higher support unlikely.

Wildlife is the property of the landowner in England. With the opportunities to hunt and to fish for game fish very limited it is not surprising that rights for hunting on good lands and for fishing for trout and salmon are quite valuable. Rights to a mile of a good salmon stream may cost up to a thousand pounds a season (Sutherland, 1968). Fishing for lower quality fish, however, is common and easily available.

The Forestry Commission

Since the Forestry Commission is now the largest landowner in England, no description of the interests of landowners would be complete without mention of it. Forestry did not become strong until World War I, when many amenity woodlands had to be felled and the country realized how dependent it was on imports. In 1919 the Forestry Commission was established and authorized to plant trees on two million acres of highland and rough grazing land, a very ambitious undertaking. The defense needs for timber reinforced the momentum of the forestry movement which tended to depreciate other interests. The result was that violent criticism was heaped on the commission for the insensitive way that its blocks of young trees were set out and fenced on the previously open, rolling highlands, denying access to walkers and greatly changing the character of the landscape. After World War II another great forest-growing effort was initiated which fell short of its goal because of competition from increased agricultural activity.

The Forestry Commission is now much more sensitive to other environmental values, and consults the National Parks Commission on its afforestation plans. This has led to better siting of plantations and a more varied tree cover. Interesting efforts have been made to reconcile forestry with amenity (Miles, 1967).

RECREATION AND HOLIDAYS

It is difficult to obtain a clear picture of recreation and holidays in England because firm statistics are limited. A fair overall impression can be gained, but detailed understanding of a certain activity or region is difficult, except where special studies have been made. But because leisure use of the countryside is so diffused it is not possible to gain more than a hint of its characteristics through formal data.

Recreation Activities

In 1965 the British Travel Association together with the University of Keele carried out the first large-scale study of recreation. It was patterned very much on the surveys of the Outdoor Recreation Resources Review Commission in the United States, and participation rates for various recreational activities can be compared with U.S. data for the same year. Several activities are included in the accompanying table which are not quite comparable, since they commonly take a somewhat different form in the United States.

PARTICIPATION IN RECREATION ACTIVITIES IN ENGLAND AND IN AMERICA, 1965

Recreation activity	Percent participating		U.S. activity, if different
	England	U.S.	
Swimming	11	48	
Walking, 5 miles or more	5	43	Walking for pleasure, with no minimum
Fishing	5	30	
Camping	4	10	
Cycling	2	16	
Natural History Study	2	14	Nature walks
Skating	1	9	
Horse riding	1	8	
Hill walking (a more strenuous type of walking)	1	7	Hiking, with a pack

SOURCES: *Pilot National Recreation Survey*, British Travel Association, 1967, p. 9. *Outdoor Recreation Trends*, Bureau of Outdoor Recreation, 1967, pp. 22–24.

The U.S. participation rates exceed the English significantly in all activities. The only one for which this conclusion is in question is the English activity "walking, 5 miles or more." The U.S. activity, "walking for pleasure," with no minimum distance specified, has very high participation rates. But a walk of 5 miles or more is a fairly long walk, and such an activity may not be so extensive in the United States; certainly it would not be the second most popular activity that it is in England, along with fishing. The relative popularity of this activity is due to the extensive footpath system, as well as to the fact that 55 percent of the households did not have a car at the time of the survey. Walking may decrease in popularity as car ownerships rise.

Day trips and holidays

Of the day trips taken in 1965, 34 percent were to the countryside, 28 percent to the seaside and 24 percent to towns (British Travel Association, 1967, p. 84). Although the countryside is the most popular, it is evident that the attraction of the sea is very strong when the distance to the coast is compared with the easier access to the countryside. It is interesting that of the 34 percent of the trips to the countryside, the report states that "only 3 percent [of the travellers] had been, or were aware that they had been, to National Parks, a value likely to have been under-reported" (p. 88), This tells something of the weak impact of the national park designation. Rarely are there signs at entrances to the parks, nor is there much other evidence of a park. Only recently have the national parks been shown on any road maps. Although many people are familiar with places such as the Lake District, the Peak District, and Snowdonia, they usually do not know of them as national parks, or think of them as being any different than places such as Devon and Cornwall on the southwest coast, which are not national parks.

Devon and Cornwall have many miles of fine coastline, and this region receives the heaviest holiday use in England. Devon has a peak visitor population of 247,000 (National Parks Commission, 1966a, p. 37), and Cornwall is inundated in much the same way. Roads to and along this part of the coast are frequently jammed for miles. Brighton, a large seaside resort south of London received

6.5 million day visitors in 1965 (National Parks Commission, 1966*b*, p. 48), and Blackpool, near Liverpool in the northwest, had 8 million (National Parks Commission, 1966*c*, p. 37). Between 65 and 70 percent of holidays are spent at least partly at the coast, and 9.5 million people spent at least part of their holiday in the countryside in 1960 (Burton, 1965, pp. 26–31). Although these figures cannot be placed on the same basis for comparison purposes, it is possible to conclude that the coast is the major holiday objective, especially the large resort areas. The use of the countryside is more dispersed, and does not center in large resorts of the sort typical of the coast.

Paid vacations of two weeks or more per year were enjoyed by 74 percent of the population in 1965 (British Travel Association 1965, p. 41), and 31 million people out of England's 48 million took holidays which averaged 10 days in length (Central Office of Information, 1968, p. 21). Data on the type of accommodation used are incomplete, but in Devon 42 percent of visitors stayed overnight in hotels, 23 percent in private houses ("Bed and Breakfast" signs are common everywhere), 14 percent in holiday flats and chalets (two types of permanent but light structures for summer use), 17 percent in caravans (trailers, the majority of which are fixed in place and rented out), and 6 percent in tents (National Parks Commission, 1966*a*, p. 37). This pattern seems to be common elsewhere in England. The number of hotel accommodations has remained fairly stable, while the use of tents and trailers has grown faster than any other type of accommodation. Trailer sites escaped control under the town and country legislation, and a number of conspicuous sites appeared in fields and pastures along the coast. In 1960 a measure of control was provided by the Caravan Sites and Control of Development Act, but not before many sites had become established.

Pressures from use of the national parks vary widely. The Pembrokeshire Coast National Park in southwest Wales is an area somewhat similar to Devon and Cornwall and is experiencing some of the same problems, especially with trailers. The Lake District faces the most difficult problems of over-use, and schemes to control traffic are being considered (Lake District Park Planning Board, 1965). As in the United States, the presence of water attracts visitors, while the high moorland parks attract mainly the hardy walkers. Thus, Dartmoor National Park in Devon attracts relatively few of the huge number of visitors that come to that county. The Peak District, on the other hand, even though it is somewhat similar to Dartmoor, attracts heavy day use because of its proximity to a number of large urban areas.

part II

A Study of Selected Decisions in the Peak District National Park

We have seen in Part I that the protection and enjoyment of the environmental resources of the English landscape relies on a complex system of traditional rights, legislation, and public supportive activities. But laws, powers, and policy are one thing; how well the system works in practice is another, and may be more important. What is actually happening to the English countryside during this era of rapid change? What direction is environmental change taking under the system, and what are the consequences for amenity?

These broad questions are difficult to answer, even in an area of prime concern such as the Peak District National Park, where this study is focused. An English national park is a far more complex entity than an American national park. Forty thousand people live within the boundaries of the Peak District National Park, and most of them work in the park. Economic activity was not curtailed when the park was established in 1951, and it has grown since. Nor was the status of land ownership changed significantly; only 300 acres of the park's total of 346,000 are owned by the national park authority, the Peak Park Planning Board. This Board functions very much as do local planning authorities all over England except that it has the additional national park responsibilities added to its planning responsibilities. (For simplicity, the term "Board" will be used hereafter for the most part instead of Peak Park Planning Board, or local planning authority or national park authority, all of which are synonomous in this case.) The proceedings of the Board bring it into direct interaction with five county councils, nine urban district councils, nine rural district councils, three river basin authorities, eleven public water supply bodies, eight regional gas or electricity boards, four economic planning councils, a number of ministries in London, and other public and private bodies. Change is as characteristic of these bodies and the people living in the park as it is elsewhere in contemporary society.

To make a comprehensive evaluation of how well the English system works in the park would require not only a measure of change in the environment but also a measure of the quality of this change. This would require objective measures of environmental quality which have not yet been developed. However, specific decisions regarding the interplay of resource use and amenities can provide important data pertinent to the question of change in the park landscape and the process of change. The study of a series of carefully selected decisions can lead toward (a) identification of the changes in the physical environment, (b) identification of the underlying forces which tend to promote change, and (c) evaluation of the ability of the planning authorities to cope with the forces of change.

Seven decisions were selected which contribute toward these objectives. Several are important decisions with long-range consequences, while others are characteristic of many decisions that the Peak Park Planning Board makes every year.

The first decision concerns the pressures for suburban residential development in the Park. It is an important decision because it forced the Board to alter its policy in a way which was not fully satisfactory but which was necessary to resist strong social and economic pressures for residential development.

The forestry case which follows illustrates a routine application of the tree preservation powers available under the town and country planning legislation, but in this case preservation was challenged by a lumber dealer who explored all available means to obtain the high-quality timber resources involved.

The protracted legal dispute over a limestone quarry is the surface manifestation of the deep conflict between the not completely irreconcilable interests of limestone production and amenity.

The water resource issue is necessarily incomplete because the actual decision is yet to be reached. The organization of water resource management on a watershed basis makes this a regional decision over which the Board's power is limited.

Three recreation decisions are studied, one involving the process of securing public access to high open land that was privately owned, and two which are concerned with the growing conflict between recreation and preservation, involving proposals for an aero-towed glider area and a trailer camp.

In each decision studied, the procedure employed was first to read the file which the Peak Park Planning Board maintains for each planning decision, including the reports of the Ministerial inspector if an inquiry was held. This information is not normally available to the public, but the Peak Park Planning Board kindly permitted me to see it. Next, the change in the landscape that followed from the decision was evaluated. Then interviews were held with the individuals or organization representatives who played important roles in reaching the decision. This was the basic data used to evaluate the underlying forces tending to promote change in the park and the ability of the planning authorities to adequately cope with the forces of change.

This method of evaluating the effectiveness of the English methods within the Peak District National Park was selected over several alternatives that were considered and rejected. One involved comparing change in and around Bakewell, the largest town in the park, with a similar town outside the park. This alternative was rejected because the Peak District towns have a very different character than the surrounding towns which have been influenced by their proximity to industrial areas and their lower elevation. Even without the national park designation, change in the Peak District would have been different from changes in the surrounding areas. A second alternative that was considered involved intensive study of an area in the park which was under particular developmental pressure, for example, for limestone quarrying or residential development; but this was rejected as leading to an unbalanced picture of preservation in the park and limiting the study to the impact of only a few resources. Early plans to perform a survey of the attitudes of landowners to public use of their land were also dropped for several reasons. Organizations such as the National Farmers' Union and the Country Landowners Association have made the position of farmers and landowners clear in numerous public statements. The displeasure of the farmers with the increasing public use of the countryside was confirmed in the case studies. The insights to be gained from an attitudinal survey were thus not significant enough to make this a central part of the study, and limitations on my time available in England precluded a survey to supplement the main effort.

5

The Peak District National Park

The geology of the Peak District has an importance for the park unmatched by any other factor. The Peak District is at the southern end of the Pennine mountains, which extend north as far as Scotland. All the region of the southern Pennines was originally covered with coal-bearing materials, but as the Pennines were uplifted these soft coal measures were weathered away. They remain, however, in the surrounding lowlands to form the great Lancashire and Yorkshire coal fields, and hence the large industrial cities which ring the park (see the accompanying figures). On the Pennines, the underlying gritstone—a hard, massive sandstone—was exposed, but in the central and southern part of the Peak District this covering of gritstone was also removed as an underlying dome of limestone was uplifted. Separating the gritstone and the limestone is a layer of shale.

The gritstone weathers quite slowly. The northern gritstone areas are the highest in the park and typically have broad summits and plateaus, covered with heather or grass moors, and with extensive bogs because of the restricted drainage. In places these areas are cut by "cloughs," rocky gullies and valleys which carry away the abundant rainfall. The highest place in the park, Kinder Scout, is only 2,088 feet above sea level, but because it is such a broad area with few distinguishing landmarks and because bad weather can come up very quickly, hikers frequently become lost and sometimes die from exposure. At the boundaries of the gritstone area are the "edges," the escarpments where the hard gritstone breaks

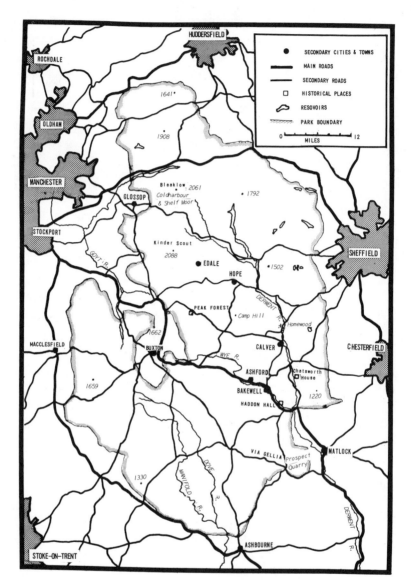

PEAK DISTRICT NATIONAL PARK

sharply to the shale and limestone valleys below and where most of the rock climbing is done.

In contrast to the harshness of the gritstone country, the limestone areas are gentle, rising to only 1,200 feet in the center of the limestone dome. The limestone country is extensively farmed, with the basis almost exclusively in grass, although heavy rainfall and limited number of sunny days make agriculture marginal, especially at the higher elevations. The limestone area is characteristically rolling, but cut here and there by the well known "dales," steep-sided valleys which were created by the widening of fissures in the limestone by solution. There are occasional cliffs, but for the most part the sides of the dales are sloping and covered with trees or grass, which add to the beauty of the rural scene. Although many of the dales are dry, others contain fine, clear streams, notably the Dove and the Manifold, which were enjoyed by Izaak Walton 300 years ago.

Largely because of the poor weather and poor farming, the villages in the heart of the Peak have changed very little from medieval times. The characteristic colors of these limestone areas are green and grey—the green of the fields and an occasional copse of trees, and the grey of the stone-built villages and stone walls around the fields. The gritstone areas, in contrast, are somber, dark, and largely uninhabited. The gritstone has a tendency to turn very dark grey after exposure to the weather. The heather and bogs are also dark. The dominant character is bleak and open on an almost oppressive scale, but since such openness is rare in England the gritstone moorlands are much frequented by hikers and naturalists.

The Peak District is full of the remains of prehistoric man. The limestone areas, like the chalk downs elsewhere in England, were inhabited and cultivated by man during the Stone Age. The Romans mined the lead found in the Peak District and built several roads through the area. Later, when the Anglo-Saxons worked at clearing the lowlands, the Peak was left to bandits and other wilder sorts of people. The Normans established firm control of the area and created the Peak Forest royal preserve. The medieval era saw the extension of cultivation and lead mining and the establishment of towns and villages very much as they are today. But the Peak remained relatively isolated because of the difficulty of travel, and it was Catholic long after the Reformation, both of which contributed to the cultural uniqueness of the region. Enclosure did not take place until the period from 1760 to 1830. It was during this time that the Duke of Devonshire reconstructed Chatsworth House and its park to their present magnificence. In 1780 the fifth duke began developing the warm springs in the town of Buxton, which soon became a fashionable spa, and the railroads also began to break down the isolation of the Peak District. The accounts of naturalists and walkers soon made it a popular area for excursions.

The Peak District saw some of the earliest phases of the industrial revolution when the fast falling streams were put to work powering mills. Textiles were the main product initially, but now manufacturing is diverse, especially in the Goyt Valley, near Buxton. For this reason it was excluded from the park, along with Buxton, because of the huge limestone quarries south of the town, even though Buxton was generally thought of as the center of the Peak District. This accounts for the deep indentation in the western boundary of the park.

The first boundaries for a park were drawn up by the Council for the Preservation of Rural England (C.P.R.E.) in Sheffield in 1939, in anticipation of the passage of national park legislation within the near future. There had been much activity in the thirties to preserve the Peak District and to secure access to the moors; and it is not surprising that the Peak District was the first national park established, in 1951, or that administrative and financial arrangements provided were as good as possible under the provisions of the National Parks and Access to the Countryside Act of 1949. The negotiations with each local authority required by the act took some time, especially regarding the boundaries, but the most serious opposition was from the counties which stood to lose planning powers over their portions of the park. About half of the park is in Derbyshire, and the Derbyshire County Council sent a deputation to London to protest its establishment. The Minister of Housing and Local Government of the Labour Government persevered, however, and set up a separate planning authority for the Peak District and one also for the Lake District National Park, but after that no further separate planning authorities were approved by the Conservative Government which replaced the Labor Government in 1951.

As provided by the National Parks and Access to the Countryside Act, two-thirds of the 27 members of the Peak Park Planning Board are appointed by the constituent county councils and one-third by the Minister. The representation from each county, and the part of the Board's cost that each county pays, was based on the area of the county in the park; Derbyshire has 8 members and pays 50 percent of the cost, Cheshire and Staffordshire each have 3 members and pay 15 percent of the cost, and West Riding of Yorkshire and the Borough of Sheffield each have 2 members and pay 10 percent of the cost. The Board was given the power of "free precept," that is, the Board is free to impose assessments on the constituent counties which the counties are required to pay. Although this caused concern at the time the Board was established, it has caused little difficulty since the county representatives, who dominate the Board two to one, are very reluctant to vote for large precepts which they will have to defend back in the county councils. In recent years, the "colour" of the county councils has changed from red to blue—Conservatives have taken over from Labour—but this has resulted in very little change in the Board's functioning and policies.

The Minister's initial nominees included several strong national park supporters, notably Colonel Haythornthwaite, a prominent member of the C.P.R.E., both in Sheffield and nationally, and Patrick Monkhouse, deputy editor of the prestigious *Manchester Guardian*. Both are still members (1969), and it was mentioned by staff members several times that these and other ministerial nominees have brought an enthusiasm to their jobs that has greatly influenced the less-committed county council members and that they are largely responsible for the energy and effectiveness of the Board. They have also provided a measure of continuity to the Board as the counties changed "colour." Recently, three ministerial appointees have been farmers, in response to criticism from the Minister of Agriculture and the National Farmers' Union that farmers were not adequately represented on the Board.

An important individual is the Board's chairman, Alderman Gratton from the Derbyshire County Council, a gruff trade-union leader who has given the Board strong and enthusiastic leadership for over 10 years. On the whole, the Board's meetings exhibit a common interest in furthering the park objectives, with little of the partisan dispute that is common in local government in the United States. The differences that do exist concern the degree to which policies should be pursued and, particularly, how much money should be spent. In this regard, it is fortunate that the park is surrounded by urban counties which have a tax base that can support expenditures for the park and to which there is a direct benefit since use of the park is predominantly by residents of the region. This is very different from parks in predominantly rural counties, where the users are mainly from distant urban areas and are not particularly welcome. The full Board meets only four times a year, and their meetings are brief. Most work is done by committees, which is the general pattern of local government in England. The Development Control Committee and the Finance and General Purpose Committees are the most important, but there are five others, dealing with access and paths, accommodations, forestry, information and interpretation, and the development plan.

The Board has also been fortunate in securing a good staff, which now numbers just under 50. The director and planning officer had served for 15 years when he recently accepted the position of director of the new Countryside Commission for Scotland. The functions of the staff are divided roughly into two parts, development control for its town and country planning act duties, and positive planning and management under the national park legislation. Town and country planning requires the services of planners with architectural, landscape architectural, and surveying skills, and the clerk of the Board, who is the legal officer. The positive powers of the national park legislation support information personnel, wardens (rangers), and a forestry crew. The central government pays 75 percent of the cost of these positions, but the fairly large administrative staff that supports both functions of the Board —development control, and positive planning—is paid for primarily by the constituent counties. Efforts to get the central government to pay for part of these costs during debate on the Countryside Act were unsuccessful.

Total expenditures of the Board during the 1967–68 fiscal year were £143,772. Of these funds, 71.8 percent came from the constituent counties and 28.2 percent from the central government (see accompanying table).

MAJOR ITEMS OF EXPENDITURE,
PEAK DISTRICT NATIONAL PARK, FISCAL YEAR 1967–68

Item	Expenditure
Administration, including development control	£86,293
Accommodations, camping and caravan sites	12,414
Car parks and pull-offs	5,134
Tree planting and preservation	5,064
Access to open country	1,983
Warden service	20,274
Publicity and information centers	11,698

SOURCE: *National Park Statistics, 1967–1968*, compiled by H. H. Full, Treasurer, Peak Park Planning Board, Derbyshire County Offices, Matlock, Derbyshire, England.

Development control is the Board's major task. In 1967–68 fiscal year, 835 applications for planning permission were received. Only 97 were refused, but of those approved, 80 percent contained conditions on their approval. Twelve appeals against the Board's refusals were brought to the Minister of Housing and Local Government, with the Board losing only two (Peak Park Planning Board, 1968, p. 11).

The Board's first development plan was completed in 1955 and the first review in 1966. The plan is the major document directing the Board's activity, and almost 100 public and private bodies were given the opportunity to review it and comment on it before it was sent to the Minister for approval. It is divided into two major parts. The first, General Planning Studies, is concerned with economic development, education, transportation, public utilities, community services, and development by the various governments involved. This is the longest part of the development plan and is very much like the plans of other planning authorities all over England, except that the special requirements of the area as a national park are incorporated throughout. The second part, Special National Park Studies, covers care of the landscape, facilities for visitors, and information and interpretive services. The plan also includes a study of Bakewell, the largest town in the park, which has special problems with housing, traffic, and parking.

It would be almost impossible to obtain good use figures for the park because of the large population living within it and the many roads which cross the boundaries. However, the general pattern is known, mainly from a British Travel Association study in 1963. Approximately 3.75 million visitors came to the park in 1963, **and**

this figure is expected to double by the early 1970s. The great majority of the visitors come for the day only. In 1963, only 35,000
stayed overnight, but this does not include those who stayed in the
hotel centers of Buxton and Matlock outside the park. Visitors
come to the park with the greatest frequency from Sheffield because it is the closest urban area; part of the borough is even in
the park. Manchester, the larger city to the west of the park, is not
only farther away but has other alternatives available in Snowdonia and the Lake District. The percentage of visitors from other
parts of England have been relatively small. There is a great diversity of activities which visitors participate in in the park, none of
which predominates except possibly driving for pleasure. Major
activities are walking, hiking, rock climbing, picnicking, nature
study, and fishing. Minor activities include spelunking, horse riding,
gliding, sailing, and grouse shooting.

One part of the British Travel Association's study asked visitors
to compare the Peak District with other holiday areas; the Lake
District, Snowdonia, and Devon and Cornwall were all felt to be
superior, but the Peak District was rated higher than the Yorkshire
Moors, a highland national park, and the Norfolk Broads, a
freshwater sports area.

VIEWS OF PEAK DISTRICT NATIONAL PARK.
(Courtesy of the Peak Park Planning Board)

LOOKING TOWARD THE GRITSTONE MOORLANDS OF THE KINDER PLATEAU.

GRITSTONE "EDGE" OR OUTCROPPING, NEAR BIRCHOVER.

GRITSTONE "EDGES." THE "ROACHES."

CASTLETON IN HOPE VALLEY. THIS IS ONE OF THE SHALE AREAS BETWEEN THE GRITSTONE
AND LIMESTONE AREAS.

TYPICAL LIMESTONE COUNTRY NEAR BUXTON.

MONK'S DALE IN THE LIMESTONE COUNTRY.

BRIDGE OVER THE WYE, IN ASHFORD-IN-THE-WATER.

6

Residential Development

The eastern side of the Peak District National Park, particularly the Derwent Valley, is under strong pressure for residential development by commuters from the cities of Sheffield and Chesterfield. (See map on p. 46.) Pressure is strongest from these cities because their eastern parts are heavily industralized, and their growth towards the west (the park side) is blocked by the Pennines, which run due north and south here. Just beyond this obstruction, however, the gritstone heights break away sharply to the Derwent Valley, which is primarily shale, and with some of the best soils and the lowest elevation in the park. Thus, people working in Sheffield or Chesterfield can drive roughly 10 miles and descend into a lush and quiet valley, escaping completely the urban-industrial environment. A number of the small villages on this side of the park lost their Peak District character during the inter-war years when planning controls were weak. Large "mock Tudor" houses were built in a dispersed pattern around these villages, a type of development the Peak Park Planning Board has effectively stopped. A short distance farther west of the Derwent Valley, as the limestone area rises in elevation, the villages exhibit very well the stone-built character typical of the Peak District. The population of the eastern side of the park is increasing because of the commuters moving in, while the rest of the park's population is decreasing slowly because of the decreasing manpower requirements of agriculture and quarrying.

The first development plan prepared by the Board did not indicate much concern for residential pressures. It was felt that the powers of the Town and Country Planning Acts would be adequate to control the spread of suburban development. However, the policy set down in the Development Plan has been the center of much difficulty, especially the clause given in italics in the key section quoted below.

> It is considered that this type of immigration will not be on a large scale, but should it have a noticeable increasing trend then the Board would regard it as contrary to the general interest of the area as a national Park. Any resulting development in the form of proposals for large units of housing will be resisted, *especially where it has no relationship to the availability of work in the locality.* (Peak Park Planning Board, 1955, p. 53 [italics added])

A housing development proposed for Cornmill Farm in the village of Calver was the key test of this policy.

THE SUBDIVISION OF CORNMILL FARM, CALVER

On March 10, 1965, an application for planning permission was submitted by a Bakewell estate agent (real estate agent), on behalf of the owner of the land, to build residences on 8.5 acres of a 38-acre farm. Although the developer was proposing a dispersed pattern of 7 or 8 houses per acre (densities often reach 20 and 30 houses per acre in England), the subdivision would still have constituted a 35 percent increase in the number of dwellings in the village, which had 187 houses in 1965. The development was designed to attract commuters; it had no relationship to the need for workers in the area, since the area was primarily agricultural. Cornmill Farm was too small to continue as an economically viable dairy unit, and the owner wished to purchase a larger farm after selling his remaining acres to an adjacent farm. Construction of the housing was to be in two phases, spread over five years.

After inspecting the site, the Board's Development Control Committee rejected both phases of the proposal. The second phase, on 4.5 acres of land, was rejected because it was outside of the village limits and would extend housing into attractive open landscape. The Board conceded that the other 4.0 acres, the first phase of the proposal, could eventually be developed since the land was within the limits of the village ("infilling" is the term commonly used for this); but planning permission was denied as being premature. Other smaller building sites within the village were available which the Board felt should be developed first, without taking up the open space of the larger site and without overloading educational facilities in the village. The Board was supported in this position by the Bakewell Rural District Council (R.D.C.), in which Calver is located.

There were additional, stronger motivations for the Board and the R.D.C. to reject this application. The R.D.C. feels responsibility —and political pressure—to provide housing for people currently living in the District. Most of these people would not be able to afford the high-priced suburban-style housing that was to be built. The R.D.C. would prefer more modest dwellings built by local people on the smaller plots of land in the village. The Board, for its part, clearly wanted to resist the growth of "bedroom communities" while still enabling park residents to obtain improved housing. The problem was that outsiders were bidding up the price of houses of modern standard in the park to the point that local residents could not afford to buy them. For both the Board and the R.D.C., the proposed development had no advantages, and for the Board especially, it promised problems in preserving the traditional character of the Peak District.

The owner appealed the Board's refusal of planning permission, and the public inquiry was held by the ministerial inspector on December 1, 1965. (For a description of appeal procedures, see Mandelker, 1962.) The estate agent pointed out that the physical characteristics of the site in question were better than the others available in the village, which explained why building had not taken place on the seven other smaller sites in the village for which planning permission existed or would be given. He also mentioned the heavy demand for low density housing of the type proposed, and that development could not be premature in view of this demand. He pointed out that an isolated row of unattractive, inter-war council houses (public housing built by the R.D.C.) screened the proposed development from the main road past the village. The Board, although mentioning the policy against immigration quoted above, centered its case on the need for a more modest rate of growth in new housing, commensurate with the scale of the village. "The first phase could result in strains on public and social services, in difficulties of social integration, and could quickly alter the character of the village."

In his report, the Minister's inspector did not specifically discuss the immigration issue, probably because the Board had not made it one of its key arguments. The inspector simply stated in his report to the Minister of Housing and Local Government that, while sustaining the Board's rejection of phase two, "the first phase of the proposed development would do no harm to the character of the village and would assist in meeting a pressing need for land capable of easy development and I see no reason why a permission in this matter should be deferred." The Minister concurred in his decision letter of February 7, 1966.

The Board was greatly concerned at the precedent that this decision might set, of accepting "land capable of easy development" as criteria for building in the national park. On March 22, 1966, a letter was sent to the Minister which finally made the Board's case explicit by emphasizing the immigration policy as fundamental to meeting the housing needs of park residents without allowing house construction on a scale large enough to satisfy existing demand and bring down prices. The reply, signed by a ministerial representative, chided the Board "to make their case . . . either at the enquiry or in written representations." It added, "The question of controlling immigration from outside the park is a wide issue and it is necessary to point out that in all cases . . . planning permission is granted in respect of the land and the occupancy of the resultant property is irrelevant."

During the same period, Mr. Peter M. Jackson, the Labour Member of Parliament from High Peak in Derbyshire, brought the issue up in the House of Commons and asked the Minister if he was aware that his Calver decision had infringed on the Board's housing policy. The Joint Parliamentary Secretary replied that the Minister supported the Board's policy of restricting development in the park and only accelerated development that the Board had accepted, while reiterating that planning control is concerned with use of land rather than with the people who use it (Parliamentary Debates, Vol. 730, p. 40). Mr. Jackson is an ardent supporter of the national parks and is on the Council of the National Trust. However, his influence on the government, as a member of Parliament, does not compare with, for example, the power of congress-

men in the United States, and he was unable to obtain any concessions from the Ministry.

Both of these indications of the Minister's position were clearly
a blow to the hopes of the Board of making its housing policy effective and far exceeded in importance the issue of the Calver site
itself. As the only option left, therefore, the Board asked the
Minister to accept a deputation to discuss the issue, which he agreed
to. On August 15, 1965 the chairman of the Board, three Board
members, the clerk (the Board's legal officer), and the planning
officer traveled to London and talked with the Minister per-
sonally. He supported a strong policy of restricting subdivisions in
the park and denied that a precedent-setting policy was involved
in the Calver decision, but again stated that discrimination against
outsiders was not acceptable. As a result of the meeting, the
Board members felt that they had the support of the Minister for
their general environmental aims in the park, and that the Minister would convey this to his inspectors, but that the problem of
housing for local residents remained unsolved. Subsequent ministerial decisions seem to have born this out. Since then, only three
out of eighteen appeals against rejected applications for residential
development have been won by the appellants, and these three
allowed only a total of three dwellings.

After winning the appeal, the owner of Cornmill Farm sold the
four acres of land with planning permission to a developer, for
the large sum of £18,500, who proceeded with the construction of
20 single-family residences and 8 "semi-detached" residences (du-
plexes). The Board exercised its usual control over design and
materials, requiring the use of artificial stone appropriate to the
locality, and slate roofing. The Board publishes a booklet, *Buildings in the Peak* (1964), which sets out its requirements on siting,
design, and materials to be employed in the park and has been
quite successful in securing conformance to it on new building. The
Board was also able to have the developer delete sun porches over
garages, but other efforts to get the developer to incorporate changes
which would make the houses less obviously suburban in appeal,
such as increasing their density, were unsuccessful. The Board
normally would have been able to exercise stronger development
control, but the adverse appeal decision restrained them in what
they felt they could require. Throughout the building process nu-

merous problems arose with the developer, not only with the Board but with the Derbyshire County Surveyor as well, whose approval of street layout and drainage was necessary. The landscape plan that the Board required was received late, and several purchasers of uncompleted residences complained to the Board that trees and bushes originally on their site had been destroyed. Because of this, the Board felt it necessary to place a Tree Preservation Order (see the following chapter) on the remaining trees on the site. The residences are presently being sold for £7,350 to £8,500, roughly twice the price of comparable residences elsewhere, which gives some idea of the attractiveness of the park environment to commuters.

For the estate agent, this had been a very profitable effort, and he is actively working on similar ventures in the park. Local people themselves are not immune to the opportunities for economic gain that housing development offers. The Board must now look very closely at applications for dwellings which farmers claim are needed for agricultural purposes since a number of these have been sold soon after construction to commuters at high prices because of their location in the open countryside. Old cottages which have been renovated also bring high prices. In some cases this is desirable, such as in the interior of the park, to prevent villages from losing population and to preserve the old houses. But in the areas within easier commuter range, this serves to reduce even the amount of low-standard housing available to local people.

For the great majority of people who work and live in the park, housing remains a pressing problem. It is common to find several generations of a family living in one house, and the great majority of houses are small. Residents' only alternative at present is to leave the area, which is difficult for many who have lived in the same village for generations. Jobs are plentiful in the eastern side of the park, particularly in Bakewell, which counters the tendency of residents to leave the area caused by the housing shortage. This problem illustrates the single most important weakness in the town and country planning legislation, the lack of positive powers to provide needed facilities. Ideally, such powers should complement the negative powers of development control.

As a result of the Calver decision, the Board has retreated from its planning obligation to provide housing for people who work in the park. It now rejects proposals for large residential developments exclusively on amenity grounds, and the Ministry has supported the Board on this. The consequences of this are desirable for the park visitor since a generally undesirable type of change is slowed, but a local resident without adequate housing would certainly disagree with this basis for evaluation. The housing problem must be solved before the preservation objective can be considered secure. The Board and the Bakewell Rural District Council are working on this problem, particularly a scheme possible under the Land Commission Act which permits councils to lease land to local residents for house building purposes with specific conditions that limit occupancy to people working in the district.

On the other hand, the Board does not seem to be concerned with the fact that it is denying owners of land suitable for residential uses the very handsome return that could be realized through development. Nor does the Board have any special concern for the people who are presently living in less desirable urban environments and who would be willing to pay high prices to be able to live in the park. The board appears to ignore these economic indicators of individual wishes in favor of the broader public objective that has been assigned to the park lands.

7

Forestry

Forestry, like agriculture, is exempt from planning control in England and Wales. This means that woods can be planted or cut down without planning permission. A felling license must be obtained from the Forestry Commission but this is to insure that good forestry practices are employed. Under the 1947 Town and Country Planning Act, however, planning authorities can issue Tree Preservation Orders (T.P.O.'s) for woods which they wish to preserve for amenity reasons. With a T.P.O. in effect, planning permission is required before felling can be carried out, so the Forestry Commission must forward applications for felling licenses to the planning authorities when a T.P.O. covers a wood. Compensation is payable only if there is a conflict between good forestry and amenity, as, for instance, when trees are allowed to become overmature and decay through a prohibition of cutting, such as a single tree in a prominent location. In a woodland, however, the objective is generally to allow limited cutting to maintain the health of the trees, while preserving the general character of the woods for which compensation is not required. The logic behind the T.P.O. when the owner of the woodland is forced to accept the financial loss that it entails is the same as for development control in general—that an individual has a certain responsibility to the rest of the community which is not compensable.

If an owner is unhappy with this restriction he has two opportunities to escape it. He can appeal to the Minister under the same appeal procedures as for appeals against development controls, or he can seek to enter into a dedication agreement with the Forestry

Commission. The system of dedication agreements is an effort by the central government to put private land into efficiently managed forests. The landowner, in return for grants to plant and maintain the trees, agrees to a forestry plan devised by the Forestry Commission. If land with a T.P.O. on it is so dedicated, the Minister of Housing and Local Government must revoke the T.P.O. This usually results in deciduous woods being clear felled and the area replanted with conifers, changing the character of the landscape significantly.

HOME WOOD, AT STOKE HALL

Home Wood is a fine, nine-acre woodland planted originally for amenity and shelter purposes directly north of Stoke Hall, a large country house rebuilt to its present form in 1750, at which time the wood was also planted. It is a long, narrow strip of oak, beech and elm between the main north-south road through the eastern side of the park, and the River Derwent. The trees are very large, with an understory of natural regeneration which has been repressed by the lack of sunlight. The effect is very attractive, whether seen from the road, the river, or the small village of Froggatt across the river. It is located in that part of the park which experienced dispersed residential development in the 1930s.

In February 1953 it came to the Board's attention that Home Wood was to be sold. A meeting of the Development Control Committee which was to have considered imposing a T.P.O. was called off because of bad weather, but the Chairman, acting for the Committee, authorized the T.P.O. and a letter was hurriedly sent to the auctioneer handling the sale asking him to declare that a T.P.O. had been authorized and to explain it. At this time it was purchased by a resident of Froggatt, who managed the wood for amenity purposes, assisted by his full-time woodman. Lumber firms did bid at this time, but how much higher they might have bid without the T.P.O. is unknown. It was not until 1957, four years later, that the T.P.O. was confirmed by the Minister; if there had been a different purchaser, it probably would have been confirmed much sooner.

In 1960, the wood's owner died and the property was again sold by auction. At the sale the existence of the T.P.O. was again announced by the auctioneer, and the Board's Forestry Officer explained that the Board would agree to only very limited cutting. On this occasion, however, the land was purchased by a timber merchant, and two months later he applied for a felling license to clear fall the wood, which was forwarded to the Board. The Board's consideration of the matter was difficult because of the possibility that compensation might result from certain courses of action, but it was finally decided to allow only a small amount of selective felling. The wood's new owner refused to accept this decision, and a site meeting was held. At this time the Board's Forestry Officer, a professional forester, suggested a 20-year period to cut most of the old growth, leaving specimen trees along the road and the river. This concession by the Board was also rejected by the timber merchant. He wished to hold the timber as a reserve against the time when he was unable to obtain enough logs on the open market to keep his sawmill working and his stocks up, and he wished to have more freedom in deciding when and where to cut. On December 30, 1960, he submitted a notice of appeal to the Minister.

The inquiry was held on November 15, 1961, almost a year later. The appellant claimed that the wood was degenerating, that about 25 percent of the timber had already been lost, and that the rest would not last for another 5 years. He rejected the Board's proposed cutting period of 20 years because of the loss it would entail, as well as the damage to the regeneration that would result from continued re-entry into the wood. He also claimed that the Board had misinterpreted the meaning of the term *clear felling*, and that only mature trees would be cut, leaving the younger trees in the open for better growth. He offered to leave specimen trees along the road and the river.

The Board accepted that the trees were mature and that growth was slow, but not that 25 percent had recently been lost and that the rest would die soon. They pointed out that most of the trees were 200 years old, and that a 20-year program of selective cutting could take the few weak trees first, but that on the whole Home Wood was a magnificent stand of trees with great amenity value. They referred to the very unfortunate appearance of other woods which had been clear felled, and pointed out that the owner was well aware of the T.P.O. when he purchased the land. The Board

was supported by fifteen individuals, nine preservation and out-
ing groups, the Froggatt Parish Council, and the present owner
of Stoke Hall, who claimed that she would have purchased the
wood herself if she thought that the T.P.O. would not be adequate
to protect it.

The Minister's inspector agreed that the majority of trees were
past maturity but felt that a 15-year time span for selective cutting would be appropriate, removing one-third of the total board
feet each 5 years. This would maintain the appearance of the
wood without the loss of the timber's value. He suggested dismissal
of the appeal, and the Minister agreed in his decision dated February 28, 1968.

The owner then sought to enter into a dedication agreement
with the Forestry Commission for Home Wood and four other parcels of land that he owned. The only recourse open to the Board
would be to purchase the property, which they tried to do. However, the owner preferred the dedication agreement to selling the
land, and was unwilling even to discuss the sale of the land at the
price that the district valuer had prepared, which was the same price
that the owner had paid for it. The Board was therefore forced
to institute the laborious compulsory purchase procedure in 1965.
During this time the Board also got in touch with the Countryside
Commission and the Ministry of Housing and Local Government,
and asked them to appeal to the Ministry of Agriculture and the
Forestry Commission to reject the dedication scheme. The only
basis for their making such a request was the ministerial appeal
decision which permitted cutting on a 15-year basis only; it is
considered to be "bad form" for one Minister to issue a decision
contrary to another Minister's. Also, Home Wood is a small wood,
much smaller that the great majority of areas under dedication
agreements, which was a factor in the Board's favor. Three years
passed before the positions were resolved between the two government agencies within the complex frameworks of several pieces of
legislation. It was not until June 1968 that the Forestry Commission sent word to the owner of Home Wood that the local planning
authority (the Board) was to handle the application for a felling
license, thus finally ceasing its consideration of the dedication
agreement.

How this decision was finally reached is not known. The timber merchant claims that he decided against the dedication agreement himself, being unwilling to hire the personnel that the Forestry Commission required under its forestry plan. At any rate, a felling license was finally issued in November 1968 for the removal of 117 trees, marked jointly by the Board's forester and the owner, the first of three cuttings spread over 15 years, just as the Minister's 1961 appeal decision had suggested. The first cutting constituted approximately one-third of the total board footage of the wood, excepting the specimen trees along the edges.

This case illustrates the difficulties that planning authorities have when dealing with the central government agencies which maintain much independence under the planning legislation. Even for this small wood, it was a long process before the Forestry Commission agreed to drop the dedication proposal, and even this may have resulted from the withdrawal of the landowner from the scheme. The appeal decision in this case was a good one and provided a sound basis for further efforts by the Board to prohibit the clear felling of the wood.

The timber merchant does not regret his purchase and has since purchased other woods with T.P.O.s on them outside of the park. One, the wood around Florence Nightingale's family house, has involved him in more troubles than Home Wood. However, the market for high-quality hardwoods is so strong that he is willing to accept the costs and risks of obtaining it from woods with T.P.O.s. Given the scarcity of timber resources in England, the outcome at Home Wood could be considered as a decision balanced between the needs for wood and amenity.

8

Mineral Extraction

Mining and quarrying are extremely important activities in the park. They provide jobs for people living in the park and they provide a source of raw materials for the surrounding industrial areas. There are over a hundred active workings, and in 1953 they provided 15.9 percent of the employment in the park, second only to agriculture and forestry with 17.8 percent (Peak Park Planning Board, 1955, p. 20). In recent years employment has declined somewhat due to mechanization of the mines and quarries.

There are almost 2,000 years of history and tradition associated with mineral extraction, particularly lead, so it cannot be said that mining is an alien element in the Peak District. Very little lead is mined today; the two major minerals extracted are limestone and the vein minerals frequently found with lead, mainly fluorspar but also barytes (the mineral form of barium sulfate). The fluorspar and barytes are obtained by working the waste heaps of old lead mines and by underground mining, both of which have a relatively low impact on the environment. The working of old waste heaps of worked-out lead mines may indeed improve the environment since the Board can require that the old excavations be filled in with waste, restoring the natural ground lines. The high value of fluorspar and its scarcity in England makes its extraction inevitable, but since this is a newer industry the Board has been able to exercise control from an earlier stage. For instance, fluorspar is processed in only one large plant in the Park, and the Board was able to have it located in Middleton Dale, where several large limestone quarries are already operating, away from roads and in a depression which fairly well keeps it out of sight, except for the settling ponds which are on level land adjacent to the depression. The major problems with the fluorspar operations are with the restoration of sites afterwards, especially by the numerous small operators.

Limestone quarrying presents a much greater problem because of the huge size of the quarries and the processing plants that occur at each one. Much of the limestone is dried or burned, both of which result in the escape of dust into the air, often to be deposited on the ground nearby. The limestone of the Peak District is of a high quality, frequently 98 percent calcium carbonate or higher. It finds many chemical and industrial uses nearby, but half is now going for construction purposes and 3 percent is still being used for agricultural purposes. Of the 13.4 million tons produced in Derbyshire in 1966, 4.1 million tons came from the park, an increase of 260 percent since 1955 (Peak Park Planning Board, 1966, p. 17).

The largest industrial operation in the park is a cement plant with a 400-foot-high stack which, with its plume of smoke, can be seen for great distances. Permission was recently given for the construction of a new plant to double the output of the cement operation. In return for this planning permission, the Board was able to obtain major concessions from the company, including the revocation of mineral rights without compensation to lands which have important amenity values, the carrying out of an extensive landscaping scheme and restrictions against the road transport of the cement. The delay that an appeal would have entailed was the main leverage the Board had in this case, but, of course, this device can only be utilized when permission is given.

In the planning for the limestone industry subsequent to the passage of the 1947 Town and Country Planning Act, the Minister of Housing and Local Government "called in" for decision at the ministerial level all of the planning permissions which were to be issued for limestone quarrying. The planning permissions were to be based on the future needs for limestone, for employment, and for the preservation of amenities in the Park, at least to a degree. The result was a series of planning permissions issued to each quarry operator specifying the conditions under which he could operate. Some effort was made to discourage production in the park in favor of the Buxton and Matlock areas which were excluded from the park partly because of the extensive quarrying. Inside the park, some efforts were made to concentrate quarrying in several locations, but permissions were given for the 24 quarries which were active at that time.

PROSPECT QUARRY

One of the smaller of these was the Prospect Quarry which had started as a wartime measure in 1942. It is located close to the Via Gellia, believed to be the route of the Roman Road through the park and still one of the major access routes. The quarry is located at the upper end of a dale through which the road passes, just before the dale opens out onto the typically open Peak District farm land. The dale is narrow at this point, so the quarry abuts directly onto the road. There are several other quarries nearby, although they are not so noticeable, and a power line passes through the area. The general condition of the farms and a small hamlet nearby is rather depressed.

In 1955 the quarry was sold. The new owners began increasing the 1950 planning permission annual output of 10,000 tons per year to 40,000 tons per year. The Board approved each of several requests for additional plant with the condition on each planning permission that by the end of 1960, or as soon as practicable thereafter, the plant was to be relocated inside the quarry, instead of adjacent to the road, and a spoil bank was to be placed and planted with trees between the road and the quarry. The Board used these planning consents as an opportunity to insert conditions in the interests of amenity, a useful device. On December 21, 1960, however, instead of relocating his plant inside the quarry, the quarry owner submitted an application for planning permission to erect a plant capable of producing 100,000 tons per year and diversifying its output. This plant would be located adjacent to the road outside of the quarry. The Board rejected the application and the owner lodged an appeal with the Minister on April 21, 1961.

At the inquiry held in November of the same year, the counsel for the appellant brought out an important point on which subsequent events turned. The original permission from the Minister in 1950 contained a condition that "the erection of plant required in connection with the treatment of the excavated limestone shall be approved by the local planning authority or the Minister." The actual intention was probably to make the plant subject to the approval of the planning authority, but the wording was equivocal. Quarrying of 17 acres was allowed in the Minister's 1950 permission and the appellant calculated that, with the proposed plant, enough stone was available for 35 years of quarrying. It was claimed that these two parts of the original permission made it mandatory that the board permit the appellant to install the new plant, and that siting the large new plant in the quarry was impossible because not enough space was available.

The Board agreed with this last point, but claimed that a large operation was never intended in the Minister's 1950 decision, and pointed to several parts of his decision letter which supported the view that the Minister simply did not want to put a small operator out of business. The Board pointed out that the new plant was to be 360 feet long and 59 feet high and in an exposed position on a major access route into the park. They maintained that the added production was not needed at that time, noted that the Minister had refused other recent requests to open or reopen quarries near the Via Gellia and in the park in general, and suggested that the appellant never intended to comply with the earlier conditions of the Board's planning permissions to resite the plant within the quarry. The Board was supported by a prominent member of the Countryside Commission, the C.P.R.E., and several other preservation organizations. Both sides called in mining and landscape consultants to support their case.

The inspector agreed with the Board that the quarry was never intended to be a large one and that landscaping could not significantly reduce the industrialization of the dale that the large plant would cause. Nor was he satisfied that the increased production was necessary or the employment. The ministerial decision rejecting the appeal was not delivered for nine months, until August 22, 1962, an extraordinarily long time, because of the necessity of evaluating the legal questions involved.

However, this case was not to end here, to the satisfaction of the Board, as would normally have been expected. The solicitor for the quarry owner was well versed in planning law and had many years of experience in mineral matters. Because planning decisions regarding quarrying involve the largest economic values of any decision the Board makes, these issues normally stimulate the most intense legal activity. In the Prospect Quarry the result was a level of legal expertise and an intensity of legal effort that the Board does not frequently have to contend with.

On September 12, 1962, only a few weeks after the appeal was rejected, the quarry owner's solicitor wrote to the Minister objecting to the decision and threatening court action. On October 11 he placed a notice of motion before the High Court of Justice in London against the Prospect Quarry decision, not on the basis of planning wisdom but on a point of law, the only type of court action the Town and Country Planning Act permits. He claimed that his client was being denied the right to operate the quarry that was provided under the terms of the Minister's original 1950 planning permission. This step immediately required that a great deal of legal work and expense be undertaken. Both sides hired legal counsel in London to handle their cases, the Board and the Ministry acting together. The clerk of the Board exhibited some concern as to how the costs would be paid if the case was lost since, in England, the losing side usually must pay the court costs.

Against the background of this legal action other activities were going on which are difficult to tie directly to the legal activities but were clearly influenced by them to some degree. A few weeks after the legal action was threatened, the planning officer met the owner of the quarry at the site, at the owner's request, to investigate alternative plant arrangements which would satisfy the Board. Soon the Board's mining consultant was brought back in to join the negotiations. On December 31, 1962, a site meeting of the Development Control Committee was held, also attended by representatives of the Ashbourne Rural District Council; at this time a plan for "limited" expansion was accepted in principle. This was two and one-half months after the notice of motion was submitted. By late 1963 the new plant was in place and a landscaping scheme was underway, and on November 14, 1963, the notice of motion was withdrawn. But it was still necessary to prepare an agreement embodying the new plan as a part of a planning permission, which had still not been issued. For some reason, this was not signed until January 9, 1969, five years later; it appears that it was a subject which the planners wished to stay away from.

In general, it appears that the Board's planning effectiveness with regard to Prospect Quarry was greatly diminished after legal proceedings began in 1963. Based on the appearance of the quarry today, the plan which the Board accepted must be judged unsatisfactory. The plant and the quarry are visible from both directions on the Via Gellia, and the six-foot bank along the roadway and its plantings required by the landscaping scheme provide very little screening. Unsightly spoil material has been deposited in both directions along the road, on which old machinery is scattered. The owner of the quarry claims that he secured virtually everything that he originally applied for; but even he lost to a degree in that the construction of his new plant was delayed almost three years, and many thousands of pounds had been spent for legal fees and for the services of consultants.

There were two main causes of the Board's failure with Prospect Quarry. The first was the defects in the original 1950 planning permission given by the Minister. The allocation of 17 acres for such a small operation was far more than was necessary, and immediately created a valuable mineral right, especially when taken with the condition that the necessary plant "shall be approved" by the planning authorities. This appears to have been merely carelessness, but it jeopardized the subsequent ability of the Board to exercise planning control. The second key was the ability of the quarry owner's lawyer to spot this weakness and to take advantage of it through court action, a step that is unusual in England because it is so greatly restricted by the planning legislation. Once the legal groundwork was taken away, the Board became unsure of what it could or could not do, which led to major concessions. The consequence is an unsightly development adjacent to a main access road in an area that needed special effort in the first place.

9

Water Resource Development

The heavy rainfall in the Peak District, which reaches 60 inches per year on its highest elevations, makes it an important catchment for the water supplies of the surrounding urban areas. But although there are 51 reservoirs in the park, of greatly varied sizes and including one which for many years was the largest in England, only three have been constructed since the park was established. Of these three, only one, the Errwood Reservoir, involved important amenity issues, and it had Parliamentary approval dating from before establishment of the park. The Board's objectives with each of these three reservoirs constructed under its planning control were to encourage good design in the dams and their associated works, to preserve the landscape of the catchment, and to secure public access and recreation on the reservoirs and the catchment.

The Board successfully reached its first objective which was to encourage good design in the engineering works. Two of the three reservoirs, the Errwood and the Lamaload, have received Civic Trust awards for good design. To achieve this has required a great deal of time-consuming work by the Board, working to gain acceptance of appropriate architectual treatments and materials, and opposing the monumental construction styles common on older dams in the park.

Progress has been made toward the Board's second aim, to preserve the landscape of the catchments, but not so much from the Board's efforts as from the slow erosion within the engineering and public health professions of the policy that the catchment must be sterilized to protect the water supplies, even when the water was to be treated. Sterilization generally meant the removal of all human habitation and of agricultural activity, and planting of conifers. The recent reservoirs constructed in the park have entailed only limited interruption of agriculture, and, where trees were planted, both deciduous and coniferous species were utilized in a design developed with the assistance of the Board's landscape architect. An important factor in the maintenance of farming on the catchment has been the pressure of the Ministry of Agriculture and the National Farmers' Union, both of which consistently oppose any loss in agricultural land. Similar efforts by the Forestry Commission to support plantations have been weakened by the very slow growth of trees much above 1,000-foot elevations in the park. One large plantation has been reclassified as a research area to study this problem.

The Board's third objective, to provide recreation in conjunction with the new reservoirs, has been initially successful, but this success is now a source of concern to the Board. Sailing is one of the fastest growing sports in England, and has been permitted on the two most recent reservoirs. The water authorities have leased sailing rights to sailing clubs formed specifically for the new reservoirs. The clubs are responsible for providing the necessary facilities and controlling the sailing, which has worked out quite well. However, spectators jamming the narrow roads leading to the reservoirs and those along the reservoirs have created problems. In one case, the Board established one-way traffic, and in both instances is trying to obtain parking and sanitary facilities. The resulting difficulties and expenses have caused them to slow down their efforts to have other reservoirs open for public water sports until additional sources of finance are obtained, since the Board does not wish to devote too much of its resources to this type of development.

Trent River Watershed

For the most part, the existing reservoirs in the park are in the gritstone and shale areas, especially in the higher areas where few people live. The limestone areas have been avoided not only because of the greater human activity in them but also because of the more difficult hydrographic characteristics of the soluble limestone, with its characteristic jointing. Several streams disappear underground when they cross into the limestone areas. Virtually all of the limestone area, however, drains into the Trent River, one of the most polluted rivers in England in its upper stretches. The Trent River Authority (T.R.A.), which is responsible for the proper development and management of the basin's water resources under the 1963 Water Resources Act, in 1968 published its *Water Resources—A Preliminary Study*. This study emphasizes the critical importance of constructing new water supply reservoirs on the Rivers Dove and Derwent, the major tributaries of the Trent River in the park.

The Trent basin is unusual in that the Trent River and two of its tributaries, the Tame and the Soar, receive massive discharges of sewage and industrial effluents near their sources, from Birmingham, Stoke-on-Trent, and Leicester. The quality of the water in these rivers is very poor, especially in the summer when flows are half of the annual mean. But after the high quality waters of the rivers Dove and Derwent are received near Derby and Nottingham, the quality of the Trent is satisfactory in the amounts of dissolved solids and nitrates it carries. The biological and chemical oxygen demands improve considerably but not enough, however, to meet water quality requirements. When future needs were considered, the T.R.A. determined that even with full development of the rivers Dove and Derwent, the water supply needs of the year 2000 cannot be met without large scale in-stream pollution control works in the Trent River itself above the confluence of the Dove and Derwent. Without these pollution controls, the Trent will be too polluted to use for water supplies. Research on several other water conservation schemes has begun, but the T.R.A. feels that additional water supplies from the Dove and Derwent will undoubtedly be essential and has announced that two new reservoirs must be completed by 1977. Seven sites are being investigated, five of which are in the park, including the two most favored by the T.R.A.

The Board has taken a cautious position on water resource development in its development plans because of the recognized importance of the heavy rainfall of the Peak District to the water supplies of the surrounding areas. Its policy is simply to "examine very critically any scheme put forward" (Peak Park Planning Board, 1966, p. 33), but this policy statement continues in a way that seems to indicate the acceptance of further water resources in the park as inevitable; it adds that the Board will "continue to press for comprehensive landscaping and for the best possible farming use of gathering grounds, and also for full recreational use of the water and catchment areas." The board has refrained from stating any further position on the reservoirs proposed by the T.R.A. until details are available.

The T.R.A.'s announcement of the need for two new reservoirs by 1977 has, however, set the wheels of opposition moving among private groups. Leading the fight is the Sheffield branch of the C.P.R.E., which played so important a role in the establishment of the park. It is also the organization that Colonel Haythorn-thwaite, a ministerial appointee on the Board since its inception, is associated with. This group has put its case before the public in an illustrated booklet titled *What Price Water* (C.P.R.E., 1968). It opposes all new reservoir construction in the park and is soliciting financial support to employ expert engineering and legal advice to this end. As alternatives to reservoirs, it proposes elimination of waste through metering of individual supplies and re-use of industrial waters, utilizing ground water storage, and pollution control, plus its main thrust of desalination plants built in conjunction with two nuclear power stations planned along the coast. All of these alternatives are in fact being considered by the T.R.A., but since the capital and research requirements of these proposals are higher, it is not surprising that the T.R.A. seeks the assured gains to be obtained from reservoir construction. The C.P.R.E. feels that the T.R.A.'s water engineers are dam builders first and do not fully evaluate other alternatives. The important amenity question which remains unanswered is the extent to which the proposed reservoirs in the park will be used for low-flow augmentation. The T.R.A. does not deny that the possibility that water from the reservoirs might be released during the summer to reduce pollution in the Trent, especially before the large pollution control works in the Trent River are constructed. Since all the reservoirs presently in the park are for water supply, the C.P.R.E. is trying to alert the public to the possibility that the new reservoirs may have unsightly muddy banks when the lake level is drawn down, and appear quite different than the existing reservoirs, which are generally full.

The C.P.R.E. by itself can only do so much, but it undoubtedly will serve to focus the opposition which is certain to be widespread, both within the park and in the surrounding areas. The decision, however, will be made primarily in London. The Water Resources Act requires that a water order for a reservoir be issued by the government in cases involving a departure from the development plan. A public enquiry must be held, at which time the Board, the C.P.R.E., and all interested parties can make their case and try to marshal as much opposition to dams as possible. However, if the T.R.A. can convince the Ministry of Housing and Local Government of its case for reservoirs in the park, the chances are that construction will proceed.

The role of the Board in the decision is likely to be minor. The Trent River watershed covers 4,029 square miles, with less than 15 percent being in the park, and its population is 5.3 million. It already receives large water imports from the west, and in the future will have to export water to Lincolnshire. Water resource development is a regional issue in which the national park is only one factor. The important question is whether national park considerations will be adequately incorporated in the decision-making process. In the introduction of its preliminary study, the T.R.A. mentions its responsibility for having adequate regard for amenities, but does not mention this subject subsequently in the study, except to say that recreation values created by the reservoir will be included in its economic model; the C.P.R.E.'s jibe, that a vast recreational resource already exists in reservoirs where public access is denied, has not registered yet. To a large degree, it will be up to the Countryside Commission to make sure that amenity issues will be adequately considered in London; the Board, the C.P.R.E., and others who view reservoirs with reluctance will have to do what they can to make the case for preservation.

10

Recreation

The establishment of the Peak District National Park did not change the status of land ownership within it. The Board, along with the Ramblers, the C.P.R.E., and others who visualized a truly "national" park, was anxious to get underway the measures available in the National Parks and Access to the Countryside Act to create the type of park they visualized. The provision of public access to open lands through the completion of access agreements was given top priority.

Approximately one-third of the park came under the act's definition of open land as "mountain, moor, heath, down, cliff or foreshore," the only type of land for which access agreements could be made. The main attractions for walkers and hikers were the high gritstone moors of the northern part of the park. The need in these areas was accentuated by the very small number of footpath right of ways in the high moors because there had been so little human activity in them in the past. These areas were also prized for their grouse shooting, and landowners and their gamekeepers were enforcing trespass laws.

The first access agreement was signed in December 1953 with the Chatsworth Trustees for 5,624 acres of land on the Kinder Plateau. This was an important first step, because by February 1955 seven other access agreements had been signed for the entire plateau, including Kinder Scout, the highest point in the park. The Chatsworth land was subsequently conveyed to the National Trust, which did not change the status of public access.

83

Coldharbour and Shelf Moors

While these agreements were being completed, negotiations were already underway for access to the Bleaklow area, just to the north of the Kinder area and very similar to it. Coldharbour and Shelf Moors were on the western part of Bleaklow, extending from the Pennine divide down to approximately 1,000 feet, where the developed grassland began. The Pennine Way long-distance route runs along the edge of these moors, along the Pennine divide. The lower part of the farm is close to the town of Glossop, and is one of the closest parts of the park to Manchester. All of the land, 1,987 acres, was in one farm which supported about 1,500 sheep.

The owner, however, was set against the idea of public access when the Board first contacted him in 1954, and further efforts by the Board to open negotiations were ignored. Subsequently, the farmer died and the farm passed to his two sons, but they had the same feelings about public access. Their intense opposition had several sources. The farm had been purchased by their father in 1945 after working a small farm as a tenant for many years and saving for the larger farm; its ownership was greatly prized. The brothers worked the farm themselves. In addition, their land contained a popular rock climbing area called Yellowslacks, and climbers frequently entered the area to climb the rocks, sometimes bothering sheep, leaving litter, and ignoring, sometimes even ridiculing, the efforts of the farmers to chase them away. There were undoubtedly walkers on the land also, but the climbers appear to have particularly antagonized the two farmers.

In the summer of 1963 the owners became so annoyed with the rock climbers that they undertook to destroy the rocks for climbing purposes by blasting them away, assisted by some friends from the local Black Powder Club. The official reason given for obtaining a blasting permit was that rocks occasionally fell away, rolled down the hill, and killed sheep, but it was a thinly disguised excuse. Headlines appeared in the local papers, and the climbers and ramblers immediately responded by pressing the Board for decisive action to save the rest of the rocks. Forty percent of the climbs which were listed in the climbers' guide had been destroyed. The Board, unable to obtain a reply to their letters from the owners of the land, wrote to their solicitor, asked for assurance that no further blasting be done until the matter could be discussed, and provided them with information and documents about access agreements. While arrangements for a meeting were still being made in February of the next year, another large charge of explosives was set off at the rocks.

Because of the attitudes of the owners and their intransigence, the Board had already instituted procedures to have an access order issued by the Ministry, and four days after the February blast, notices were sent the local governments of nearby areas, the National Parks Commission, and the Ministry of Agriculture, asking for their positions on the placing of an access order on the land. In the Derbyshire County Council, the Conservative minority lined up behind a group of hill farmers who had announced to a number of newspapers the organization of a revolt against the "dictatorial practices" of the Peak Park Planning Board regarding the rights of farmers. Chaper-en-le-Frith Rural District Council refused to approve the access order until the terms of the order were made known. Rather surprisingly, the Minister of Agriculture supported the order, as did the National Parks Commission, Glossop, and Manchester.

The local opposition, especially from the organized group of farmers, made it appear that the Board's access program was in difficulty. However, the powerful National Farmers' Union (N.F.U.) did not support the revolt and, in fact, played a very constructive role in blunting it by recommending to the farmers that they talk rather than fight. When the Board's clerk finally managed to meet with the owners of Coldharbour and Shelf Moors in May, the N.F.U. had agreed to provide counsel for them. The Derbyshire County Secretary of the N.F.U. assisted them through the negotiations, and this service was paid for by a grant from the Countryside Commission, as provided for under the terms of the National Parks and Access to the Countryside Act. By August 1964 the first draft of an access agreement had already been prepared and, although much patient negotiating remained, the threat of an access order had served its purpose of forcing the owners to negotiate. With an agreement, the farmers could influence the terms of the agreement, instead of having to accept an order as the Board devised it.

The case that the N.F.U. could put to the farmers toward this
end was a good one. It may have proceeded in this way. "People are
going to come onto your land anyway; you would have to hire
several helpers to keep them off. You might as well sign an agreement, get a little income from it, and, most importantly, have the
park's warden service patrol your land and keep an eye on the
rock climbers and the ramblers, making sure that they keep their
dogs under control and that they don't worry your sheep. The
warden service can only operate on land that the public has access
to. They will put up signs, and when your shooting tenants want to
shoot, the wardens will inform the public who will then have to
stay off your land, although you have to let them know ahead of
time when shooting is to be done."

By early 1965 negotiations were almost complete but the N.F.U.
was now bargaining for as much as possible for the farmers. This
was the first negotiation that the N.F.U. was involved in, and
they saw it as an opportunity to secure favorable terms which
would provide a model for subsequent agreements. Earlier agreements had largely been signed with landowners who, the N.F.U.
felt, did not have adequate regard for their tenants. The agreement
for Coldharbour and Shelf Moors, along with several others on
Bleaklow which were being negotiated at the same time, required
that dogs had to be on a leash instead of "under control" as in
the previous agreements; allowed only two access points to the
lower boundary of the access land instead of the four that the
Board would have liked; excluded several parcels of low-lying land
which the farmers claimed were improved land, or soon to be improved, and thus not within the definition of open land; and permitted 12 days per year when the moors could be closed for shooting, instead of the usual 10 days. But compensation was the main
bargaining issue. It was finally agreed that £15 was to be paid by
the Board each year for each mile of boundary stone walls and
£7.10s for each mile of interior stone walls, for a total of £37 for
Coldharbour and Shelf Moors. The Board wanted this to commute
their liability for damage from public use, but the farmers would
not accept this; the agreement as signed left the farmers the right
to make additional claims for damages from public access. In fact,
a supplemental payment was agreed to in 1969, allowing the
farmers an additional £5 for each 100 ewes, for another £37.10s per

year. Such payments, small though they are, are a big improvement over the former compensation provisions which require that the owner had to show that losses had occurred, which is difficult to do. No payments have been made to landowners under the earlier agreements for losses suffered from public access, although there is general agreement that such losses do occur (mainly from stone walls being knocked down and from dogs running sheep into stone walls or causing them to panic).

The agreement for Coldharbour and Shelf Moors was completed and signed by the Minister on March 17, 1965. The owners are now thoroughly satisfied with it. They are on excellent terms with the Board and the wardens, although they still exhibit antagonism to certain types of rock climbers and even to the mountain rescue group which serves the park, many of whom are rock climbers. Of the concessions the N.F.U. obtained during the negotiations, only the limited number of access points has caused any trouble; walkers still use a rather obvious access point which they do not have a right to do. The Countryside Commission has incorporated the method of compensation developed in these negotiations in the standard access agreement form which it recommends to public authorities.

The Board now finds access agreements much easier to negotiate than before. The limited funds for warden services, rather than opposition from landowners, is holding up further agreements. The value of the warden service to farmers was impressively demonstrated in 1968 when the wardens enforced the restrictions on public access to the park during the epidemic of foot and mouth disease. There were only very minor outbreaks in the park compared to the surrounding areas, for which the warden service received much credit and good will from the farmers. The Board employs four full-time wardens, 100 part-time wardens who work on weekends mainly, and about the same number of volunteer wardens, although the trend is away from voluntary service because it is difficult to organize and is somewhat less dependable. During the 1967–68 fiscal year, £20,274 was spent for the warden service while only £1,987 went for access, and much of that was for signing. Normally the figures are somewhat less, but foot and mouth disease entailed additional expenditures that year.

At present, twenty access agreements cover 75 square miles, or 14 percent, of the park, and access is also permitted on an additional 18 square miles of National Trust land. It would not be correct to say that farmers now welcome visitors; they still find them annoying and would much prefer to be left in peace; but once they accept that public use is inevitable and likely to increase in the future, the advantages of an access agreement become obvious. Even so, it requires patience and tact on the Board's part during the negotiations—a very different type of task than their development control efforts—to maintain discussions on a subject which the farmers find basically distasteful. The satisfied holder of an agreement has often been the Board's best asset in a negotiation, but it was largely through the efforts of the N.F.U. that the terms of the access agreement have become much more appealing to the farmers.

AERO-TOWED GLIDING

On November 2, 1961 the Derbyshire and Lancashire Gliding Club submitted a request for planning permission for the "use of existing agricultural land for occasional flying purposes in conjunction with the normal gliding activities of the Club." The site was on Stanley Moor Farm in an agricultural area in the Parish of Great Hucklow, near the geographical center of the Park. It is only about a mile from the club's Camphill gliding site, which is in a depression on the top of a broad hill and well out of sight. At Camphill, however, the terms of the club's lease permitted winch launching of gliders only, in which a long cable attached to a winch pulls the gliders into the air. The club attempted to have the terms of the lease changed but the landowner's refusal was unconditional out of the fear that grouse shooting on the nearby Abney Moor might be disturbed by the noise of the towing aircraft. The club then obtained an option on the Stanley Moor Farm (which is not moor at all but improved grass), and submitted the request for planning permission.

The Derbyshire and Lancashire Gliding Club is one of the oldest and most respected gliding clubs in England and has operated the Camphill site since 1935. It has pioneered new techniques and contributed significantly to meteorological knowledge about air movements. From the end of World War II until 1954 the National Gliding Championships were held at Camphill, which is a spectacular site, but since then the championships have been held elsewhere where aero-towing was available. It was claimed that aero-towing, in which a light plane tows the glider as high as desired, was necessary if the club was to remain viable. The secretary of the club, in the application and in several subsequent letters to the Board, stated that only a small number of flights would be made from the Stanley Moor site, which would remain in agricultural use, and that spectators would be discouraged. The Stanley Moor site was to be entirely ancillary to Camphill, where a large parking area was available and the club's headquarters were located, but where, it was claimed, conditions were unsuitable for aero-towing.

The Development Control Committee met officers of the club on the site and listened to these arguments. Except for Colonel Haythornthwaite and the planning officer, there was a general feeling in favor of granting the permission. During the subsequent meeting a week later, however, it was decided to advertise the proposal in the Derbyshire newspapers for a week in view of the local concern that was developing over the issue. Interested parties were asked to respond by January 8, 1962, and a flurry of activity followed as both sides solicited support.

Fifteen letters in support of granting permission were received by the clerk of the Board, mainly from gliding and aviation supporters but also from the Royal Meteorological Society, sports groups, and the Bakewell Rural District Council, within whose jurisdiction the site is located. In opposition were the four parish councils in the area, 74 local petitioners, a general petition with 216 signatures, numerous preservation groups, the National Farmer's Union, and the Countryside Commission. The most active opposition was from nearby residents who accepted the silent gliders but objected to the noise of aircraft in the quiet rural environment, the spectators it would attract, the resulting traffic on the narrow country lanes, the littering, and the possibility that activity on the site could increase in the future beyond what the club officials foresaw at the time. This last fear was reinforced by the landowner of the Camphill site, who felt that the club was violating the spirit if not the letter of their lease by using an adjacent site for aero-towing.

The impression was given that if permission were given and aero-towing initiated, the landowner might not renew the club's Camp-hill lease when it came up for renewal in 1964, throwing all club activities to the Stanley Moor site. The preservationists generally claimed that aero-towing was incompatible with national park objectives, and they brought out that there were no other airfields in the park.

The meeting of the Development Control Committee on January 9 found the members undecided, so two steps were taken. An offer by the club to put on a demonstration of aero-towing outside of the park was accepted, and the committee decided that the full Board should decide the issue because of the wide public interest. By this time a number of newspaper articles had appeared, and some notable public figures had entered the debate. In addition, the planning officer was to step up a survey he had initiated of other aero-towing sites and the type of problems that had occurred.

The demonstration was carried out in very poor weather on January 31. It was attended by about 60 persons, including 12 members of the Board, 6 members of the Bakewell Rural District Council, and a dozen members of the press, in addition to the officers of the gliding club. The demonstration itself evidently did little to help the Board members make up their minds, nor did the survey of other aero-towing sites, where few problems had arisen. But the process of public and private debate and discussion finally led to the decision by the full Board on February 13 to refuse the permission. The reasons for refusal sent to the club were to preserve the peaceful, unspoiled character of the area against noise and spectator activity, to avoid the problems which might result from the low standard of roads in the area and the possible future increase in use, and finally, to prevent the inappropriate use of a national park. Out of respect for the club's good name, the Board would have liked to have given the permission, but there were too many problems, present and potential, standing in the way.

Shortly after, the club's option to the Stanley Moor Farm expired. The property was subsequently sold at a public auction; the club was the high bidder, and the Board began preparing for the appeal which was then sure to follow. The public inquiry was held on September 5, 1962, and produced few statements that departed from those already heard by the Board. One important change, though, was that the Bakewell Rural District Council called back its support of the club's proposal for further consideration and remained undecided at the time of the inquiry. The club thus lost the only local government support it had. The Minister's inspector agreed generally with the Board's decision, and the Minister's decision which followed did also.

The effect of the rejection of the club's application cannot be fully known, but clearly the club is still active and growing, although no recent national championships have been held at Camphill. The club's steward did not seem to feel that the rejection was too much of a setback. Resentment against the decision was also reduced when the club sold the Stanley Moor Farm for an excellent profit. In retrospect, the Board's carefully made decision must be considered correct.

THE ASHFORD CARAVAN SITE

It is the policy of the Peak Park Planning Board to encourage the provision of camping and caravan (trailer) sites in the park on a limited and strictly controlled basis. There are a number of caravan sites that were established before the Board had adequate power to control them, but there is a strong tendency for the caravan sites to go into static uses, either by the rental of fixed trailers to visitors on a weekly or seasonal basis, or as housing on a permanent basis because of the housing shortage in the park. This leaves few spaces for touring caravans. The policy on the development plan favored the provision of small informal caravan sites for up to six touring caravans, managed by the landowner or the tenant. Large commercial sites were to be discouraged as "not a particularly appropriate use of land in a national park, and it is felt that sites of this kind, if needed, should be located on the edges of the Park" (Peak Park Planning Board, 1955, p. 87). The difficulties with this policy were well illustrated in the decision concerning a caravan site near the fine old village of Ashford-in-the-Water, near Bakewell, to be developed by the Chatsworth Trustees for the Duke of Devonshire.

The Duke no longer controls the vast portions of the Peak District as former dukes once did, death duties having taken their toll. But the integrity of the family home, Chatsworth House, has been

maintained, and it is one of the most famous stately houses in England, set in a 2,500-acre park designed by Capability Brown. Revenue from visitors to Chatsworth is important to the Duke's ability
to retain ownership of it. The Duke was said to have asked that the
proposed caravan site be a showpiece for other developers in the
park.

The agent of the Chatsworth Trustees approached the Board
late in 1961 about developing a model caravan site on the Duke's
land somewhere within the Peak Park. The Board considered this
a good opportunity to secure a well-developed and well-managed site
to help provide for touring caravans. The staff of the Board assisted Chatsworth personnel in the canvassing of possible sites
and the selection of a proposed site on the edge of the well-preserved
village of Ashford-in-the-Water, only a mile from Bakewell and
just inside the boundary of the Bakewell Urban District.

In May 1961 an application was submitted for a 65-site
caravan development on 8 acres of a 30-acre site. The remainder
of the site was to be left in agricultural use, possibly to support a
pony riding concession later, which the Board was also encouraging as a valid park activity. The site was not visible from the village or the trunk road which passes through the village because the
site was on higher ground, out of the river valley. It also was
screened from the north by a band of trees, but it could be seen
from higher ground to the south. The leasee agreed to plant 10- or
12-year-old trees as part of a landscaping scheme.

The proposal was explained to members of the Bakewell Urban
District Council (U.D.C.), in which the site was located, and the
Bakewell Rural District Council (R.D.C.), in which most of the
village of Ashford is located, by members of the Board and the
Chatsworth agent during a site meeting on May 24. The Board is
generally on good terms with most district councils in the park; the
Bakewell U.D.C. is one of the exceptions. The ill will stems from
the time of the establishment of the park when the Board took up
powers formerly exercised by the U.D.C. At the site meeting one
councilor was indignant that the U.D.C. had not been contacted
earlier in the process of finding a site, especially since the U.D.C.
would probably have to provide the utilities. The Board's clerk,
their legal counsel, stated that consultation was not appropriate

until after an application for planning permission had been made. The councilor suggested that the Board was already committed to the site, which the Board denied while restating the policy of encouraging sites for touring caravans. When the subject of utilities came up the U.D.C.'s surveyor said that the water system in the area did not have enough pressure to supply the site, and the U.D.C.'s Medical Officer of Health confirmed one councilor's statement that septic tank treatment of sewage would not be acceptable and that a long sewer line would have to be constructed, even though the village of Ashford itself depended wholly on septic tanks. Many other problems were considered, which the Board felt could be handled by suitable conditions on the planning permission. The members of the other council involved, the R.D.C., especially those from the Ashford area, stated that their objections were completely on amenity grounds. At the close of the meeting, a U.D.C. councilor suggested that the caravan site should be located on part of Chatsworth Park, the park designed by Capability Brown around Chatsworth House!

Subsequently, opposition to the caravan site centered around the residents of Ashford, where a petition was circulated and was signed by 260 people, 220 from Ashford out of a village population of 590. The Board felt it advisable to call a public meeting, which was held in the Ashford Parish Hall on the evening of July 27, at which 76 people signed the attendance sheet. Although the Board and the Chatsworth agent put their case as well as they could, the proposal was effectively criticized. The fairly large, commercial nature of the development did not fit very well with the statements in the Board's development plan about providing small sites. In response to questions, neither the representatives of the Board or of Chatsworth were willing to give assurance that the site would never be increased over 65 sites, mainly since they could not speak for persons in their same positions in the future. This did little to allay the fears of the villagers that the operation would grow in the future. When the proposed caravan site was fully occupied, its population would be almost half that of the village as a whole; the effect of this many additional people on the village, the Wye River, which runs through it, and its grassy banks was projected, regardless of the merits of the operator. Several landowners described violations of their property rights that had already occurred in conjunction with the public right of way along the river from Ashford to Bakewell. And an application for two houses on a site near the proposed caravan site had been rejected by the Board, partly on the grounds of the poor junction of the access road with the trunk road through the area, the same access road that would be used by caravans to reach the site. All in all, the high standards and good intentions of the Board and Chatsworth were effectively tarnished for the villagers, and strenuous appeals were put forth to the Board to look for an alternate site outside the park, in accordance with the development plan.

The Board found itself in a difficult position. Dealings with the Chatsworth Estate frequently caused an undercurrent of talk among local people about the ability of the Duke to get what he wanted, as was certainly the case in past centuries. In actual fact, the Board has denied several applications submitted by the Chatsworth Estate, although, for the most part, the environmental objectives of the Duke and the Board are very similar. And there was a public need for good sites for touring caravans; the Board was forced to provide one itself near Castleton for 40 caravans in the popular Hope Valley–Edale area. The Board's policy of encouraging small informal sites had not been effective for several reasons. Such units were rarely economic to operate and were hard for visitors to find. Indiscriminate use of informal sites during peak periods had also caused some trouble. What was needed to meet the legitimate needs of visitors with caravans was precisely the type of site being proposed, and the Ashford site was a good one in many ways. It would have good facilities and be well-managed, and a responsible landowner and operator are key factors in this field which frequently attracts poor management with inadequate capital.

Therefore, the Board decided to issue the planning permission on November 15, after considering the question for some time. The permission contained fourteen conditions which were adopted after careful study of what could be done to reduce as many of the problems that the villagers had pointed out without discouraging the development altogether. The site was to be occupied from March 1 to October 31 only, to make sure no residential use developed. The surrounding woodlands owned by Chatsworth Estate were to be managed for amenity purposes, and a landscaping plan approved by the Board was to be completed before the site could be used. The access road was to be improved and the utilities would require the approval of the Board in addition to the usual U.D.C. approval.

It was the U.D.C.'s utility requirements which now (1969) have delayed the construction of this caravan site, probably until 1970, when a new sewage collection system is to reach Ashford. The developer was reluctant to undertake the large expenditure for sewerage that was otherwise required by the U.D.C. The Chatsworth agent feels that if the site had been in the Bakewell Rural District instead of the Urban District, septic tank disposal would have been acceptable and the site would have been in operation for several years.

The Parish Council of Ashford-in-the-Water would have liked very much to appeal the Board's decision, but this alternative was not available to them. An appeal can only be made against planning refusal or the conditions of a permission, and not by a third party. This denies a body like the Ashford Parish Council a right to appeal, but it also keeps innumerable other third parties from appealing planning decisions, which would certainly result in an overwhelming number of appeals.

These last two decisions regarding recreational development illustrate the conflicts between amenity and recreation, uses which are frequently compatible until recreational use increases to the point of interfering with amenity. In many ways the preservation of a rural environment is similar to the preservation of a wilderness environment; the introduction of a discordant use, even a minor one, can interfere with the dominant character of the environment. A quarry has much the same effect on an otherwise completely rural scene as it does on an otherwise wilderness scene. The effect of aero-towed gliders or a trailer camp on the agricultural landscape of the Peak District National Park is probably very similar to the effect of a helicopter operating in a wilderness area. In each case, the returns from such uses have to be weighed against the environmental loss. But the point at which a recreational use ceases to be profitable in this calculation is a difficult point to identify. In these two cases, the Board wisely asked for advice from the public, which it then used in making its decision. But in both cases it relied on its own deliberations to arrive at a decision, over-ruling public opposition on the caravan site and accepting it on the aero-towed gliding proposal.

All three of these cases also show the Board acting in areas where its jurisdiction is virtually complete, save for the possibility of an appeal, a significant difference from the situations regarding water resource development, mineral extraction and forestry, where their control is incomplete.

11

Deciding the Environmental Issues of the Peak

Change in the physical environment

Of the seven decisions considered here, five have resulted in, or will result in, change in the physical environment, and one is still undecided. Only the rejection of the aero-towed gliding proposal left the environment unchanged. This is roughly comparable with the rate at which the Board approves planning permissions for the park in general: 88 percent of the 835 applications submitted to the Board in the 1967–68 fiscal year were approved and will lead to change.

The quality of the changes in the environment

In one case, Prospect Quarry, it can be said safely that the quality of the environment deteriorated as a result of the decision that was made. The additional limestone produced could have been obtained with greater efficiency and less environmental disturbance from one of the larger quarries in the park, instead of expanding a small quarry and its plant adjacent to a major access route into the park. On the other hand, the access to Coldharbour and Shelf Moors added to the environmental resources available to the public with only the minor damage to plant life that is generally agreed to accompany public access to moorland.

Between these two extremes, however, are four other decisions, evaluation of which would require some method of weighing the benefits of change against the environmental losses. Does the pleasure of the new residents' living in the village of Calver rather than in an industrial city compensate for the rapid infilling of the village and the strain on its social services? Is the controlled removal of old growth timber from Home Wood compared to natural aging processes an acceptable price to pay for the wood products obtained? Will the enjoyment of people staying in the trailer camp near Ashford compensate for the disturbances to the villagers and the sight of trailers in the field as seen from one direction only? And should reservoirs be constructed, or should other types of water conservation works be undertaken with greater risk, greater cost, or both? These are questions which cannot be decided objectively until adequate measures of environmental quality are developed. These cases, involving comparisons of gains and losses of both physical and social values illustrate how complex environmental questions are. But these cases were decided, and it is appropriate to attempt to identify the major factors which influenced the decisions.

Change in the park originates in a group of strong social forces, mainly for good places to live, for jobs, and for resources, including preserved environments. These forces represent the search for the good life in a changing world. They are the moving forces; the governmental activities that follow are in response to them. No legislation or governmental body should be strong enough to deny these forces, but only to respond to them and organize them in a way that is as satisfactory as possible.

THE PEAK PARK PLANNING BOARD

The Board's major powers to organize these forces are negative, the denying of planning permission under the town and country planning legislation. The fact that these are negative powers greatly influences everything the Board does and the way it does them. It has very limited powers to initiate change in a direction of its own choosing. What powers it has stem from the national park legislation; but only a very small part of the Board's activities are directed toward improving the physical environment. Some derelict buildings are removed and approximately 10 percent of powerlines are being put underground by the electricity boards; but the meagerness of funds available severely limits these programs. For the most part, the Board fights what is essentially a rear guard action against

physical changes in the landscape while trying to provide for legitimate social change.

The pragmatic nature of the Board's actions

To help to secure acceptance of its decisions the Board would
like the public to think of it as applying normative, incontestable
"principles of good planning" in reaching its decisions. If this
were what the Board did, however, it would seem that it would be
most evident in cases in which its powers were most complete and
the social forces involved least intense. The two recreation cases,
for the aero-towed glider site and the trailer site, should thus illustrate the Board applying its planning wisdom to reach the decisions; but in fact the Board relied to a large degree on expressions
of public feeling in both of these cases.

Where the Board does apply its "principles of good planning" consistently is in its resistance to the stronger forces tending toward
large-scale change, such as residential housing and quarrying. With
a limited ability to control these changes, the Board relies on its
"principles" to support the correctness of its decision against the
developer, whose motives the Board can disparage as being incon-
sistent with its "principles." The Board's policies, as set down in
the development plans, generally oppose those forces leading toward physical change in the landscape and support those elements
which maintain the traditional character of the Peak District,
such as agriculture and stately homes. But there is little the Board
can do with its negative powers to ameliorate the largely economic
problems of agriculture and stately homes. What the Board can do,
however, with its negative powers is to control the physical changes
which stem from the active forces. Thus, the objective of most of
the Board's work is obvious: to minimize physical change. Because
of this, most of its activities involve deciding on strategy. Sometimes
the strategies are successful, as when the deputation was sent to
the Minister to object to his housing decision. Sometimes they fail,
as when the Board tried to secure a compromise at Prospect Quarry
to avoid a difficult court case. But the strategy the Board uses in
the majority of its decisions is to rely on its invincible planning
wisdom, especially when dealing with the less sophisticated appli-
cants for planning permission.

The minor role of economic analysis

Economic forces are definitely among the most important with which the Board has to deal; but even though they are often manifestations of basic social forces, as for housing in the park, they are not accorded special status as "value free" indicators of the public will that they often are in the United States. Planners on the Board's staff could point to no instance where an economic analysis was carried out to help to determine whether the cost of a preservation measure was worthwhile. Although a subjective weighing of benefits and costs may well be a part of the decisions made by individual Board members, these benefit-cost considerations rarely pass from the subjective to the objective. For instance, in answer to a question about the extra cost to build with natural or reconstructed stone, a planner replied simply that the question was irrelevant because no other material was "correct" in the Peak District. The cost of most preservation measures taken in the park is paid for by owners of the resources for which full utilization is denied, as in the case of quarrying or residential construction, or by those who must employ higher standards, as when special landscape treatment is required. Of the seven cases studied, only the one involving access to the moors failed to illustrate this characteristic; in this case a small payment was made to the farmers as compensation for the costs resulting from public access. In the other cases, however, the Board attempted and sometimes succeeded in restricting development without explicit consideration of the cost to the resource owner.

In a sense, this characteristic avoidance of economic factors could be considered as an illustration of the pragmatic nature of the Board's efforts. As mentioned previously, the Board does not have the positive powers necessary to influence many of the forces acting within the park, forces which are perhaps most clearly indicated by economic supply and demand data. The Board cannot reduce the demand for housing, for timber products, or for minerals. Because of this situation the Board seems to avoid these economic factors which it cannot influence, emphasizing instead the powers that it does have to control development. The result is that the economic basis of many problems is disregarded, and the assumption is made that the application of "principles of good planning" will resolve the issues properly. As a practical device for gaining the Board's objectives, this strategy is probably quite functional. A consequence, however, is that the costs of preservation are born disproportionately, and there is no specific effort to have those who benefit most pay for the preservation.

THE MINISTRY OF HOUSING AND LOCAL GOVERNMENT

The Ministry also has the same broad responsibility as the Board, but it is above the Board in the planning hierarchy and sometimes must overrule the Board on regional and national considerations. For the most part, however, the Ministry supports the Board's objectives. The greater problem from the central government is the distortion to balanced consideration of issues caused by the agencies which are exempt from planning control. This situation is analogous to the separate federal agencies in the United States, with their organizational rivalries and the resulting inefficiencies and conflicting programs.

THE NATIONAL PARKS AND ACCESS TO THE COUNTRYSIDE ACT

The main contribution of this legislation is to place the national park objectives into the framework of the town and country planning machinery, thus enabling the Board to raise its standards of environmental preservation somewhat higher in the Peak District than would be possible without the national park designation. However, other attractive areas not in national parks employ similar standards. The increment of preservation stemming from the national park designation is hard to identify; it may be small since preservation is given very high priority by the residents of many attractive parts of rural England. The positive measures made possible by the act would require a much higher level of financial support than is presently available before the national park designation could result in significantly better standards of visitor services, leisure opportunities, and removal of non-conforming uses.

In none of the decisions studied was the role of the Countryside Commission important. The Town and Country Planning Act is the key to the preservation of the environmental resources, and the

Board and the Ministry hold the planning powers as well as the major responsibilities under the act.

LONG-RANGE PROSPECTS FOR PRESERVATION—A PERSONAL EVALUATION

The Peak District National Park, like other areas in England, contains a human element which national parks in the United States often lack, and which compensates for the absence of grandeur and wildness in England. In the least disturbed parts of the Peak District there is a harmony in the way that the natural environment is infused with the works of man, especially in the way that the old villages and farms fit into the landscape. Add to this the attractiveness of the natural landscape, with its gentleness and intimacy, and the result is very satisfying. It is an environment which directs the observer's interest (as natural areas do not) to history, folk art and architecture, human ecology, and varying life styles.

Unfortunately, many of the traditional human elements of the Peak are anachronisms; as they slowly decay, the organic wholeness of the environment will decline also. Farms will be consolidated, old farm buildings will lie derelict near large efficient metal structures, and mines and quarries will be further mechanized; light industry will be encouraged to replace the jobs lost, but young people will still leave and the vacant cottages will deteriorate or be bought by mobile outsiders; the tightly knit, traditionally oriented social structure will break up and give way to contemporary culture. The presence of the commuter or the former city dweller in the Peak is symbolic of this revolutionary change; a fairly good measure of the progress of this change would be the change in kinship patterns across the park. There is a world of difference separating the prosperous, educated and worldly commuters from the countryman who is more interested in the price of milk or fluorspar than the view, who considers wildlife vermin, and who is only interested in preservation when it pertains to his own interests. However, it is the countryman who must have had a strong aesthetic sense to fit these elements together so well, who is responsible for the harmony of the scene as it exists today. The commuter, even if he is a preservationist and more interested in the arts, is bringing change with his higher standard of living and

greater demands for services and for use of the physical environment.

On the whole, however, the change in the park landscape will be
small compared to the break-up of the social patterns which
shaped it in the first place. There is little that the Board could or
should do to influence this social change; it will concentrate instead on minimizing the concomitant physical changes in the
landscape as much as possible. At best, the cottages will be
spruced up, flowers planted, and additional services provided (as
has happened in villages all over England). The villages and
farms will still be attractive, but they will not have the organic
wholeness that is the result of form following function. Preservation of an English national park, with its extensive yet subtle human elements, is far more difficult than preserving the natural
environments in the usual type of national park.

For the vast majority of people, the Peak Park will remain an
extraordinarily attractive place to visit. Most casual visitors will
not be aware of the differences between remote areas of the park
and areas where outside influences are stronger, because the Peak
Park Planning Board has held the changes in the physical environment close to the minimum possible.

12

Conclusions

There are six major conclusions that can be drawn from this study of the evolution of the English system of providing leisure use of private lands and of the way the system actually functions in the Peak District National Park.

1. The system does in fact rely extensively on use of private land to satisfy recreational and leisure needs. Expenditures by the central government for these needs in rural areas have been very small, and most local governments spend virtually nothing. In fact, some groups, especially the preservationists, complain that the government carries this policy too far. They claim that the government should adopt more positive measures to enhance the countryside; and farmers feel the government should provide more intensively developed recreation areas instead of encouraging further recreational use of agricultural areas. The government, realizing that the potential for increased public use of private land is limited, passed the Countryside Act in 1968 and initiated the policy of providing country parks to supplement recreation on private land.

2. Many high-quality leisure and recreational opportunities are provided under the English system. Throughout most of England there are extensive areas of attractive rural countryside which offer many opportunities for walking, driving, picnicking, nature study, and other uses; and the restrictions on urban sprawl make the distance to the countryside relatively short except in the largest urban areas. The opportunities available in the countryside are primarily for a low-intensity type of use. More intensive recreational opportunities, which can be provided economically by the private sector, are characteristic of resorts along the coast and of

recreational developments in urban areas. In the countryside, most services for camping areas, trailer parks, and food, for example, are also provided by private operators, although in some cases, mainly in the national parks, the government has provided information and interpretive services to facilitate public use of the countryside.

3. The town and country planning legislation is the foundation on which preservation of the rural environmental resource rests, and one of the foundations on which public recreational use of rural areas is based. Preservation is accomplished primarily through the requirement that permission must be obtained from the planning authorities before development of land can be undertaken. This is a powerful tool, but the fact that it is negative in character has a tremendous influence on the outcome of its application. Undesired developments can often be prohibited, which is a significant accomplishment, but the underlying social forces causing change cannot be directly influenced, nor can desired developments be provided. The National Park and Access to the Countryside Act of 1949 provided some very limited positive powers, but the national park designation has provided only limited increases in environmental preservation and enhancement because of the administrative and financial arrangements incorporated in the act. The act did, however, place the national park objectives within the planning machinery.

4. Public support for the planning controls is very strong in England. The major responsibility for effectuating the controls rests with the local governments; this gives the numerous local preservation and recreation groups ample opportunity to work for their objectives. In addition to these activists, however, there is a wide interest within the community for environmental matters, stimulated by the extensive public discussions of planning issues. Public opinion is mainly on the side of maintaining an attractive environment, and governmental and private bodies looking for sites for needed developments often stand alone against a solid front of local opposition. The fundamental difficulty is that finding a good place for necessary developments is often impossible, and landscapes must often be marred in ways which everyone agrees are unfortunate, as, for example, by powerline and highway construction, when there are no fully satisfactory alternatives. England, unlike the United States, must export goods to survive; and efficient

transportation, power production, and resource development cannot be compromised too far if England is to remain competitive with other European countries.

5. The cost of the preservation achieved under the town and country planning acts is sometimes high, even though the government does not pay the cost. Full utilization of land and resources is often denied in the interest of environmental amenities, and the government provides no compensation to owners for these restrictions. Instead, since the Land Commission Act was passed in 1967, the government taxes heavily the increase in the value of land that results from giving permission to develop land. A portion of the costs that landowners initially pay is subsequently borne by the public in higher land costs and in higher building costs necessitated by the higher architectural standards imposed by planning authorities. On the other hand, the planning controls could be seen as reducing the external diseconomies that would otherwise have resulted from uncontrolled development. The English, however, do not look at this question from an economic point of view. The controls are considered to be restrictions on what an individual can do with his land in the interests of broader community values.

6. The ability of the English system to meet the needs of the future is by no means sure. As mentioned above, country parks are to be provided to supplement the leisure use of private land in the countryside. As demands on preserved rural lands grow, the quantity of such lands diminish. The population is growing, old housing is being replaced at lower densities which require more space, highways are being constructed to accommodate the growing number of cars, economic growth requires more resources, and traditional farming techniques are being replaced by an industrialized agriculture. How these demands can be met in the long run is difficult to say; the outlook is rather bleak. However, the planning machinery to deal with these problems is strong, and there is widespread support for preserving the English countryside. Because of these two favorable factors, the probability of achieving a standard of preservation fairly near the maximum that is possible, consistent with growth, is high. Even so, this does not change the overall trend, which is toward greater environmental pressures and a decrease in the environmental resources on which public leisure use of the English countryside is based.

part **III**

Usefulness of the English Methods
in the United States

13

Can America Benefit from the English Experience?

It is difficult to determine whether a system that has worked in one country might work in another. Although much of the heritage of the United States stems from England, many other countries have influenced our culture, and the tremendous size of the United States compared to England, and our unique historical experiences have molded a special American character. Our partially English heritage does not assure that the English system can be successfully transplanted to the United States today. Yet the question of whether we might reap some of the environmental benefits of the English system is directly relevant to our own open space and recreational problems. For this reason, it may be useful to consider some of the factors that may hold back efforts in the United States to secure land-use controls comparable to those of England's town and country planning. This is done primarily by looking at the outcome of various efforts to secure stronger land-use controls in the United States.

An American observer of the town and country planning processes in England soon notices two factors which are very different from those in the United States. One is the different attitudes toward land and its use, and the other is the flexibility of the parliamentary system in establishing strong planning powers compared to our constitutional system.

It is not surprising that there are basic differences in our attitudes toward land; we have a vast amount of land and a short history, while England has a great deal of history and little land. For centuries, England has lived under the restraints of a small, densely populated and intensively utilized country. During much of its recorded history it has been overpopulated at existing levels of technology. In the Anglo-Saxon and medieval eras community control of land use was necessary to assure the well-being of the community. Later, following the enclosure movement, ownership of land became the difference between life with dignity and a level of poverty that frequently included homelessness, begging, and stealing. The industrial revolution and the agricultural depressions of the nineteenth century broke the importance of land ownership as the major determinant of welfare, but the conditions that workers and their families lived in in the industrial cities served to maintain the desire for country life. Today, there is a pervasive demand for land in the countryside that cannot be satisfied, and which finds its expression in political support for the preservation of the traditional appearance of the rural landscape. Considered as such a valuable resource, it is not surprising that conservation measures to protect it, such as the town and country planning legislation, are widely accepted even though they involve deep incursions into the freedom of an individual to do what he wants with his land. Historically, however, it does not appear so radical, but appears to be simply the reintroduction of the age-old community control of land that was interrupted by the enclosure movement.

By contrast, during most of our history, land in the United States has been available in a seemingly unending supply. It could be purchased inexpensively, squatted on, and finally obtained free under the Homestead Act. One distinguished historian has presented the thesis that abundance is the most important single determinant of the American national character (Potter, 1954). We have been able to leave undesirable land and environments, to quit farm lands which had become infertile and woodlands which had been logged for greener land beyond, and to escape from the deteriorating central city to the suburbs. The English do not think of these as alternatives as naturally as we do and are forced to take care of the land they have. In the United States, the vast abundance of land has hindered attempts to justify limitations on the freedom of individuals to use land.

The concept of providing leisure opportunities on private lands also may be more functional in England because of the diversity of natural features, richness of human elements, and dense population within easy access distance of the preserved landscapes there. These factors have promoted a system which secures the efficient and intense utilization of a high-quality resource. In this country, on the other hand, the human elements are less diverse, and although the quality of many of our natural features is very high, they are dispersed over such a large geographical area that access is more difficult. Generally, our landscapes lack the diversity and intimacy of the English countryside. Also, our countryside does not have the extensive system of public right of ways and common lands that England has. The leisure benefits of applying English town and country planning techniques in the United States (if this could be done) would certainly be great, but probably not as great as the benefits that have been obtained in England.

But there are a number of fast-growing metropolitan areas in the United States where population characteristics are becoming similar to England's and where ecologic and land-use problems are already severe. Might not proposals for stronger land-use controls find an increasingly favorable response here? The opportunity to restrict industrial activity if it cannot be accommodated safely, to control urban sprawl, and to establish clear boundaries between city and country are strong incentives. Yet here the second major difference with England comes into play in the form of constitutional limitations applied on land-use controls stronger than zoning.

Under the federal system, control of land use is reserved to the states, which have delegated it extensively to local governments. Except on federally-owned land, Congress does not have the power to bring about planning legislation that could be applied on a comprehensive basis in the way that Parliament was able to require town and country planning throughout England. Barring a constitutional amendment, more effective land-use controls will have to be developed largely by state and local governments.

This does not mean that the federal government's role will be unimportant. There are extensive areas in the United States that remain in the public domain and under federal control. In addition, many federal programs greatly influence land use, such as Federal Housing Administration home mortgages and freeway construction. But such activities are divided among many federal agencies and often lead in different directions and frequently to undesirable consequences for the environment. A proposal for a national land-use policy currently before Congress is aimed specifically at resolving these conflicting federal programs, and also to influence state and local government policies by denying or providing funds. (To cite a recent example, federal control of funds was used to help prevent construction in Florida's Everglades, a development project that had been strongly protested by conservationists.) And then there are the important federal regulatory powers, based on the power to control interstate commerce, that have great influence on air and water pollution, electric power production, transportation, and navigation. Despite such federal influence, however, it will still be up to state and local governments to look comprehensively at their total environment and channel change into satisfying patterns, including the diverse components contributed by federal programs.

But even an enlightened local government with good public support may not be able to establish land-use controls as strong as those in England because of other constitutional limitations that are presently in effect. The power to impose regulatory measures is known as the police power. It is defined only in the most general terms as the power to foster public health, safety, morals, and the general welfare through regulation. The police power is limited in many ways by the constitution but primarily by the due process requirement of the Fourteenth Amendment, which reads, in part, "No state shall . . . deprive any person of life, liberty, or property without the process of law; nor deny to any person within its jurisdiction the equal protection of the laws." Through a long series of court decisions this requirement has been interpreted in ways that would almost certainly result in an "unconstitutional" verdict if English methods were applied by a local government today and contested in court.

The major limitation is that property cannot be taken for public uses without paying compensation to the owner. Whether a land use control measure is a valid exercise of the police power to regulate land use or is actually a taking of the rights to land for public use has been the crux of many court cases, but in no cases have courts upheld zoning of private land for the purpose of preserving open space unless there were extenuating circumstances, such as obvious health or safety hazards which made development hazardous, as in flood plain zoning. Normally, open space lands must be purchased by the public under the power of eminent domain. The cost of obtaining a benefit must be paid by all the community, not by requiring one individual to bear all the cost. With rapidly increasing land costs and the financial difficulties that are so characteristic of local governments, the result of this requirement— very little acquisition of new park land and virtually no large scale open space programs—could have been foretold. No scheme, no matter how ingenious, can avoid this requirement. Even the National Park Service, with the superior financial resources of the federal government behind it, has found it very difficult to cope with rising land costs. Point Reyes National Seashore is perhaps the classic example of the almost impossible task facing any government trying to preserve an environment by purchasing it.

An intermediate device, between regulation and the purchase of the full title to land, is the acquisition of easements to obtain only the development rights of land to maintain present uses. This has met with some success, especially in rural areas where development values are low. Wisconsin has used easements extensively to protect parkway roadsides. Around urban areas, however, the development values frequently approach the cost of the full title, reducing the usefulness of easements. It is the avoidance of these heavy costs that characterizes the English system, and which is the focus of this study.

The second major limitation on the police power is that a regulation must be consistent, treating similarly situated property owners in the same way. This would make it very difficult, for instance, to establish a distinct town limit, where the houses would end and the countryside begins, because adjacent property owners would be treated quite differently. One owner could realize the increased value of residential uses while the other would be forced to leave his land in agricultural uses. Although zoning frequently results in different treatment of neighboring properties, as between commercial and residential uses, it has not been employed to deny any form of development.

Equality of treatment could be obtained by taxing away the increased value realized on the land that was developed, thus leaving owners of developed and undeveloped land in a similar financial position. But even the English could not carry off this severe a concept and had to settle for a betterment levy of half of the development value that was realized, dividing the gain with the developer while leaving the owner of undeveloped land with no compensation. It is unfortunate that meeting this constitutional requirement of equality of treatment would necessitate such a radical provision. In its favor, however, is a sound and important justification; the development values were created by the growth of the community in the first place, and therefore the community should benefit from the values created at least in part. A speculator, unless he improves the land, contributes no real public benefits for his financial gain. A heavy tax on development values realized by a speculator tends to discourage speculation. Immediately after 1947 when England was taxing away all of the development values that had been realized, a shortage of land was a major problem since a profit could not be made in developing land. This is in extreme contrast to the United States, where with favorable capital gains taxation on the profits of land, we have encouraged speculators to offer too much land, causing leap-frog developments in very dispersed patterns and putting heavy strains on public utilities and services.

The third requirement on the use of the police power is that the restrictions must bear a reasonable relation to the purpose of the restriction. Esthetics is only slowly being accepted as a valid purpose to be served by zoning, compared to long-established purposes such as the protection of public health, safety, and morals. The amount of legal fiction has at times become ludicrous when two acre housing plots were justified primarily as protection of the public health. This is changing now as protection of the environment is gaining acceptance as a part of the general welfare. This is most clearly illustrated in the acceptance of billboard regulation without compensation on the basis of esthetics rather than the dubious safety arguments. The difficulty of including esthetic considerations in zoning, however, is primarily practical. Legislators find it very difficult to legislatively define esthetic standards, and courts generally are reluctant to do the job since it is properly a legislative function. Because ours has been a government by laws, not men (as a safeguard against the arbitrary use of power), there has also been a reluctance to assign the task of evaluating esthetic factors to governmental administrators without also providing legislative standards.

SOME AMERICAN EXAMPLES OF EFFORTS TO CONTROL LAND USE

The problems encountered during efforts to protect landscapes in the United States illustrate the operation of these limitations. There are some successes, especially when there is a fortuitous combination of landowners and government, but land-use control schemes that are applicable without these key elements have either been unobtainable legally or excessively expensive. The following examples of effort to control land use are ones that have proceeded far enough so that their usefulness, legality, and public acceptance can be evaluated.

Mill Creek, Pennsylvania.

In 1942, a group of residents along Mill Creek in the township of Lower Merion on the fringe of Philadelphia foresaw that development of their largely natural residential area was inevitable under existing zoning and land-use controls. They prepared the Mill Creek Conservation Agreement, a perpetual restrictive covenant to preserve the area very much as it was in 1942, and obtained the signatures of the owners of 68 percent of the property along the creek. It established a conservation area averaging 250 feet wide and several miles in length along the river and the road which parallels it. Hiking by the public is permitted along the creek but no other recreational activities, although the public road is a very pleasant drive. Of the other 32 percent of the land for which the covenant was not signed, some parcels of land have been broken up and sold as smaller lots, although not to the extent that the predominantly natural character of the area was changed. Many non-signers have abided by the terms of the agreement also. Values of the land with the covenant have generally kept pace with the values of unrestricted land. The township officials, who assisted the property owners in originating the scheme, are hoping to apply it in other areas in the township, and it is considered to be a very successful program (Matuszeski, 1966).

Lake George, New York

Under a 1964 statute of the New York legislature, small groups
of property owners can establish zoning ordinances if a petition
for the zoning is signed by the owners of two-thirds of the assessed
valuation of the property in the area concerned. This provision
has been utilized in four areas along the east side of Lake George
in the Adirondack mountains, an attractive summer home area.
The zoning has limited objectives; commercial development can
be prohibited, but not further construction of summer homes. The
major idea was to prohibit the type of strip commercial development that had occurred along the west side of the lake adjacent to
the state highway. The majority of the residents of the zoned east
side of the lake are from metropolitan areas, are relatively affluent,
and are willing to forego the realization of the commercial value
of their property for the enjoyment of a quiet lakeside atmosphere
(Eveleth, 1966). There are no public recreational facilities on the
east side of the lake, and a long time resident of the area felt that
the residents would probably oppose the provision of public facilities.

The zoning ordinances in New York could be removed in the
same way they were created. This is a possibility, especially towards
the southern end of the lake where the commercial values of the
property are rising. Once this land is purchased by commercial interests, they would soon be able to push opposition to the zoning
over the one-third of the property value ownership necessary to re-
move the zoning ordinance.

Upper East Branch of Brandywine Creek, Pennsylvania

This ambitious program has greater implications for wide application than the Mill Creek and Lake George techniques
since it lacked the element of relatively affluent landowners. The
scheme proposed to the residents of this rural area, some 35 miles
from Philadelphia, was that they should voluntarily sell to the
Chester County Water Resources Agency the development rights of
the flood plain and 300 foot-wide strips of land on both sides of
the flood plains and also the steep slopes and wooded areas of the
Upper East Branch watershed. This would total some 46 percent

of the 37 square mile area and cost an estimated 2 million dollars. The objective was to preserve the water resources of the area and to preserve environmental values as suburban development occurs. The population of the area is expected to increase rapidly from the present level of 4,200 people. A very comprehensive study was made and an attractive brochure was sent to the landowners (Chester County Water Resources Authority, 1968), explaining the scheme carefully and the benefits it was to provide. However, the suspicious nature of the residents towards government was such that the plan was rejected in six of the eight counties involved; it was therefore not undertaken. Some residents were only willing to lease their development rights so that the lease value would rise with general land values and property could be sold at higher prices. Many residents openly questioned why outsiders were interested in their area, and a common fear was that it was some type of recreation scheme which would attract undesirable outsiders.

The residents seem to respond to two motivations. One, they truly like the quiet rural life, and two, they look forward to selling their land for a good price when suburban development approaches, perhaps moving farther out to repeat the process. On this basis, trying to preserve their present area makes no sense; it is much easier and more profitable to move once in a while.

The Green Spring and Worthington Valleys, Baltimore County, Maryland

This area, referred to as the Valleys, has some of the same elements as Brandywine, but here the landowners were anxious to protect this exceptionally attractive landscape. The appearance of the land and the attitudes of owners are both rather English in character. Ownership of some of the large parcels of land extends back two centuries, and maintenance of the land is considered more a family responsibility than an individual economic venture. To complete the image of England, the Grand National Steeplechase is held in the area annually.

However, the Valleys are on the edge of the expanding Baltimore metropolitan area. Baltimore's beltways and expressways establish the boundary of the Valleys area, and the population of the 70-

square-mile area is expected to increase from 17,000 in 1962 to 110,-
000 in thirty years. To provide for this growth with the least possible
environmental losses, two bodies were formed, a voluntary citizens
planning council, to develop a plan for the area, and a real estate
syndicate, to distribute the development values that were realized
equitably to all land owners, including those whose land was to be
left undeveloped. Through the plan for the Valleys (McHarg, 1969,
p. 79), development was directed to areas where high density residential communities could be accepted, on the plateau areas primarily,
leaving the Valleys and their wooded slopes unchanged. Development values realized by this method were felt to be greater than
through suburban development of the entire area. Full co-opera-
tion was received from the county, the only governmental jurisdiction involved, which reinforced the plan by not providing sewerage
in the valleys and by establishing appropriate zoning. This is one
of the most successful efforts and indicates what can be accomplished
under ideal circumstances.

The California Land Conservation Act, 1964

This act was approved by statewide vote after a great deal of
public interest and debate, and it was hailed as a major advance
in controlling the spread of subdivisions over prime agricultural
land. It provided that taxes on land formally accepted as agricultural preserves would be assessed on the basis of agricultural
use rather than market value. It was designed to overcome the
common tendency of high taxes to force land from agricultural to
residential uses. The act required that preserves be left in agricultural use for ten years after notice of termination is given by the
landowner, after which the land could be sold for development
without penalty. This has been the major weakness of the bill; in
effect, it reduced the cost of holding land for speculative purposes.
And even with low taxes, farmers found it hard to refrain from
selling land for what must be considered a fortune compared to
the returns from agricultural uses.

But there have been other problems as well. Loss of tax revenues
has put strains on local taxing units, particularly school districts.
Lost tax revenue generally must be made up by higher taxes on
adjacent land not in agricultural preserves, which causes opposi-

tion to their establishment. A similar law in Nevada was declared unconstitutional as not being equal in its impact (Griffin, 1968, p. 194). The amount of tax reduction varies considerably depending on development values and assessing policy, but it can be significant, up to 80 percent. Thus, the cost for a temporary benefit can be high. Some planners suggest that it is more of a tax break for farmers than an open-space measure. Preserves often are randomly located, without conforming with important public values or open space plans, and 80 percent of the land in preserves in 1969 was more than 10 miles from the nearest city (Joint Committee on Open Space Land, 1969, p. 47). No public use, other than visual, is provided. The conclusion seems inescapable that the lost taxes could have been put to better and more permanent investments in purchasing land or scenic easements. Modifications are being undertaken to tighten up the provisions of the act, primarily to permit a longer period of reservation; the major consequence of these modifications will probably be to reduce landowner interest in preserves.

In certain areas where preservation of agriculture conforms with the long-term interests of landowners, the program has been more successful. The prime example is Napa Valley, north of San Francisco, where superior quality wine grapes are grown by the descendents of the European immigrants who first brought plant stocks and winemaking skills to California. They have readily accepted the preserves even with virtually no tax savings in order to resist the incursions of housing into the vineyards. But such "irrational" economic behavior is not very common, and the question arises of whether future generations will have the same regard for the land in the face of high prices offered by home builders as the towns in the area continue to grow.

Agriculture Zoning

A number of states have authorized the use of this device in which minimum lot sizes for houses of 5 to 25 acres are required. This is usually adequate to discourage building of houses, although not always. Whether such zoning is strong enough to halt suburban sprawl is doubtful at present since it would be denying too much of the economic value of land compared to adjacent land used for housing. A foremost legal expert on open space issues feels that agricultural zoning in urban places "appears unlikely to withstand development pressures" (Strong, 1965, p. 32). Residential development of large lots that are zoned agricultural is certainly undesirable because it removes the rural character from large areas with very little benefit provided in volume of housing. For the purpose of open space preservation at this time of rapidly increasing population, higher housing densities should be a major objective.

State Zoning

Hawaii applies state zoning to all land. The state government has capitalized on a unique situation in which one-third of the land is owned by the government and one-half by ten large trusts and agricultural corporations (Wenkam, 1967, p. 33). Under an ownership pattern such as this, landowners and the government can cooperate in imposing strong zoning controls with much less concern for the effects falling disproportionately. The local governments have strenuously objected to zoning for agriculture and conservation (the latter to protect watersheds, soils, forests, and scenery), but the combined power of the state, the landed estates, and urban conservationists has been fairly successful so far in withstanding pressures against zoning for these purposes. However, the intense pressure that rapid growth is generating, particularly around Honolulu, is becoming so difficult to resist that the state is now seeking a federal grant to study European methods of controlling land use.

In theory, state zoning offers substantial advantages over local government zoning. Growth can be planned on a statewide basis, diverting developments away from problem areas to parts of the state were they can be accommodated, avoiding the very constricted range of alternatives available to local governments. In practice, this type of planning may be largely an exercise in futility unless devices are available to force development in conformance with the plan. This has been the great problem with planning in the United States in general; the planners propose but economic and political factors dispose—frequently in very different directions. The trend to larger and larger urban glomerations will be very difficult to stop. A large urban area, even with all its environmental problems, still offers advantages as an industrial location, mainly a large market, a large labor force, and a full spectrum of transportation facilities. England, even with strong planning powers, has still had to spend large sums to direct industries away from London.

For the most part, zoning has been a very weak device for influencing development, and has served primarily to apply some organization, but not discouragement, to the growth of urban areas. It could possibly direct development away from crop lands or high amenity areas to land better suited for development, but a deep wedge of green space into an urban area, or a green belt around an urban area, could not be maintained under present limitations. For the most part, the use of zoning in the United States has been a far cry from what it theoretically could accomplish. For instance, a recent court decision in Michigan ruled that an ordinance prohibiting trailer parks in a rural area was invalid, claiming that no one would be adversely affected and there was no relationship to public health, safety, and welfare (American Society of Planning Officials, 1970). The National Park Service has combined zoning with the threat of purchase to secure control of private land in Cape Cod National Seashore. The zoning prohibits development of any land in the Seashore, which is very strong zoning, indeed; but the threat of purchase if development is undertaken is somewhat hollow owing to the frequent lack of funds to purchase such lands.

PROSPECTS FOR SUCCESS

The examples of success among these recent efforts appear to be associated with characteristics which are of very limited occurrence in the United States. First, they generally involve areas with landowners who are either relatively affluent or else have a special respect for the land, as in Philadelphia's Mill Creek, the Valleys of Baltimore County, and Napa Valley in California. The absence of this most important component spelled failure or, at best, very limited gains. Second, large parcels of land are a distinct advantage in that they put the consideration of losses and gains in a larger context, reducing the inequality of treatment which is difficult to avoid with small plots. And third, the presence of only one governmental jurisdiction greatly facilitates the co-ordination of all aspects of development controls toward an agreed-upon plan, reinforcing the effect of control devices that by themselves would not be very strong.

Successful programs were primarily private efforts to secure private objectives rather than to create public values, although important public values were created in several instances. Specific efforts to secure public values through compensation in the absence of favorable owner attitudes had limited success. In the Brandywine effort, the landowners' fears of public use of the land was an important factor in their decision not to sell the development rights to their land. Under the California Land Conservation Act, payment in the form of a tax concession secured a limited public value for a limited period, and at a relatively high cost for the benefit obtained. The scenic easement, which is the most logical form for controls that are stronger than police power regulations, has been employed extensively by several states; but relying on scenic easement to effect comprehensive land-use planning would be impossibly expensive, especially around urban areas where land use problems are most severe.

Thus, in considering ways that are presently available to obtain the comprehensive land use controls that characterize English town and country planning, we see that legal requirements force the innovations back into the molds of established techniques; into zoning, which is weak; or into the purchase of certain rights to land, which is expensive. These legal requirements, however, should not be made a scapegoat; to a large extent they are a reflection of traditional American values. But this is precisely the reason why it is not correct to be too pessimistic about the future. Public attitudes about the environment and its protection are changing, and legal requirements can be expected to change with them. The law is not static, the Constitution and the Bill of Rights not excepted. The great merit of the Constitution has been that it has been flexible enough to provide for the changing needs of this country through new Supreme Court interpretations. Public opinion is a basic element in this process; the Supreme Court leads, but it is also led. This is how the relationship is described by a noted legal scholar, Carl Brent Swisher in *The Supreme Court in Its Modern Role*:

The Supreme Court is able to lead in constitutional development, then, only by virtue of the fact that its leadership is of such a character that the people and their representatives are willing to follow. To put the matter more simply, the Supreme Court succeeds in leading largely to the extent of its skill not merely as a leader but as a follower. Since the medium of its leadership is the law, or the decision of cases in terms of the law, we can go further and say that the effectiveness of the Court's leadership is measured by its ability to articulate deep convictions of need and deep patterns of desire on the part of the people in such a way that the people, who might not have been able to be similarly articulate, will recognize the judicial statement as essentially their own. The court must sense the synthesis of desire for both continuity and change and make the desired synthesis the express pattern of each decision (Swisher, 1958, pp. 179–80).

That attitudes are changing on a broad front is clearly reflected in the heightened responsiveness of federal and state legislatures to environmental problems, the efforts of students, lawyers and other ecological activists, and the attention given to the problems in the media. Even groups who have in the past opposed strong governmental intervention in private activities have readily accepted the need to place limitations on the pollution of air and water. And although the attitudes toward private property are of a more fundamental nature, it should be remembered that zoning itself was a revolutionary restriction on private property until the Supreme Court ruled it valid in 1926. The previous device, of suing parties who caused nuisances to adjacent property owners, had become inadequate to cope with burgeoning cities and increasing land use conflicts; the situation today is certainly analogous.

Because of the critical nature of our problems, in which questions of survival are becoming more and more prevalent, the entire legal area is in a state of flux. There are signs that we are beginning to realize that how we use land is a basic element in the generation of pollution and all of the other problems, social and biological, that come under the heading of the ecological crisis. At present, methods to cope with these trends are minimal. In California there is an organized effort to halt the construction of the last stages of the California Water Plan because of the realization that southern California cannot cope with the further population growth that so much additional water would permit. Unfortunately, this is a very imperfect device to accomplish better population distribution. The extraordinary aspect of this illustration is that some people in the Los Angeles area have finally come to realize that further growth will mean more traffic, pollution, monotonous suburbs, and crowded beaches, rather than only increased prosperity, as it has been seen in the past.

But because the origin of environmental problems frequently lies with large segments of our economy (and thus with the public), politically acceptable schemes to improve them are difficult to develop. A constitutional amendment to permit a system comparable to English town and country planning would almost certainly run into bitter political opposition. Even so, such a proposal could provide a focus for groups concerned with the environment and might stimulate state and local governments to take more effective action, even if the amendment did not pass.

The more likely way in which comprehensive land use planning and stronger land use controls could be obtained is through the Supreme Court. The most important changes in the fabric of American institutions since World War II have been made by the Supreme Court, particularly the ruling on school desegregation in 1954 and the one-man one-vote ruling in 1962; it is unlikely that these significant changes could have been accomplished through the political process. There are several sections of the Constitution that could be utilized to express what has been learned about man and his environment and to balance the restraints on land-use controls that present court interpretations entail. Probably the most obvious is the Ninth Amendment, which states, "The enumeration in the Constitution of certain rights shall not be construed to deny or disparage others retained by the people." Is not the right to a decent and livable environment one of the most fundamental to life itself? Both the Fifth and Fourteenth Amendments provide protections of life and liberty, as well as property. Perhaps the time has come when property will cease to receive such inordinate concern in favor of other aspects of life and liberty that are being impaired by a rapidly declining quality of the environment.

Each of these constitutional amendments offer legal bases on which to argue for stronger land use controls. But what form could such new controls take that would enable them to restrict the seemingly inexorable growth of urban areas and their ultimate consolidation into a megalopolis? One form suggested by English experience is the initiation in this country of a tax on the increased value of land that results from up-zoning agricultural land to more intensive uses. At present up-zoning results in substantial windfall profits to landowners, profits that were not created by any productive activity of the landowner but by the general process of urban expansion. A development tax of, say, fifty percent of the increased land value that was realized following up-zoning, would have two desirable effects. One is that some of the profits would be taken out of land speculation while at the same time generating tax revenue that could be used to purchase public recreation land. The second effect, and potentially the more important one, would be that such a development tax would reduce the inequality of treatment between land that is developed following up-zoning and land for which up-zoning is denied. In other words, such a development tax would reduce the constitutional objection to open space or agricultural zoning by halving the inequality in treatment of adjacent landowners on different sides of the boundary between city and green belt. When such a tax measure is supplemented by the application of the 9th Amendment to protect the rights of citizens to healthy air, water, and green spaces, we may be able to achieve the long range goal of directing development away from our already over-large metropolitan areas and towards other areas that can absorb further development.

Land use controls such as this, or any new type of controls, would have to be achieved first by city or county legislation, including perhaps the passage of state enabling legislation. After it was put into effect, this probably would be followed by a suit to test the constitutionality of the control measure. With favorable rulings, preferably upon appeal to the Supreme Court, the control measure would be legitimized for use elsewhere in the U.S. Financial assistance for the long political and legal processes might be obtained from foundations that are presently supporting activities in the environmental field. The extensive English experience with town and country planning is an invaluable resource to draw upon in the effort that we must make to secure for ourselves and our descendents a decent and satisfying environment.

However, it should be remembered that England, even with its strong powers, has not been able to solve the problems of rapidly growing urban areas, at least not to the degree that they have been able to solve land use problems in rural areas. In both countries there is a common discontent with the conditions of urban life. Land use controls and planning must be seen within the context of powerful economic forces that are shaping not only our country but urban industrialized societies the world over, forces that are extremely difficult to resist. At present most people believe that we must continue to encourage economic growth to maintain full employment and general economic health. This is a national objective that has very wide support; but it entails increasing consumption of energy and resources and expanded use of transportation networks. Economic forces are also motivating the continued movement of industries to the already too large urban areas where environmental problems are generally the most severe. At the same time our population continues to grow, and more jobs, homes and land continue to be needed. In the long run, it is these basic forces motivating our national life that must be altered. Land-use controls cannot be expected to make them disappear, especially when jobs are threatened or individual freedoms given up without compensations in the form of a more satisfying environment. It is not only in land-use controls that American society is going to change profoundly if we are to come through our ecological crisis and achieve a stable and enduring relationship with our environment. Major changes in our attitudes toward life and in the way these attitudes are reflected in our institutions will be required. The future will depend on how well we can cope with change.

References

Addison Committee, *Report of the National Park Committee.* Cmd. 3851. London: His Majesty's Stationery Office, 1931.

American Society of Planning Officials. "Edwards vs Township of Montrose." *Zoning Bulletin,* February 1970, p. 5.

Barlow Commission. *Report of the Royal Commission on the Distribution of Industrial Population.* Cmd. 6153. London: His Majesty's Stationery Office, 1940.

Blenkinsop, Arthur. "The National Parks of England and Wales." *Planning Outlook* 6 (1965): 9–75.

Bracey, H. E. *Industry in the Countryside: The Report of a Preliminary Inquiry for the Royal Society of Arts.* London: Faber and Faber, Ltd., 1963.

British Travel Association. *The Pilot National Recreation Survey.* Report No. 1. London: British Travel Association, 1967.

British Travel Association and Social Surveys (Gallup Poll) Ltd. *Social Survey of the Peak District National Park.* London: British Travel Association, 1963.

Buchanan, C. *South Hampshire Study: The New Forest.* Supplementary Volume II. London: Her Majesty's Stationery Office, 1966.

Bureau of Outdoor Recreation. *Outdoor Recreation Trends.* Washington, D.C.: U.S. Government Printing Office, 1967.

Burton, T. L., and Wibberley, G. P., *Outdoor Recreation in the British Countryside.* Studies in Rural Land Use, Report No. 5. Department of Economics, Wye College, University of London, 1965.

Central Office of Information. *Britain: An Official Handbook.* London: Her Majesty's Stationery Office, 1968.

Chester County Water Resources Authority. *The Brandywine Plan.* Chester County, Pennsylvania, 1968.

Council for the Preservation of Rural England. *What Price Water?* Voluntary Joint Committee for the Peak District National Park, 22 Endcliffe Crescent, Sheffield, England, 1968.

Country Landowner [Journal of the Country Landowner's Association, London], April 1968, p. 101.

Cullingworth, J. B. *Town and Country Planning in England and Wales.* Revised edition, London: George Allen and Unwin, 1967.

Dower, John. *National Parks in England and Wales.* Cmd. 6628. London: His Majesty's Stationery Office, 1945.

Edwards, Kenneth C. *The Peak District.* London: Collins Clear-Type Press, 1962.

Eveleth, Peter Ames. "New Techniques to Preserve Areas of Scenic Attraction in Established Rural-Residential Communities—the Lake George Approach." *Syracuse Law Review,* Fall, 1966, pp. 37–48.

Fedden, Robin. *The Continuing Purpose.* London: Longmans, Green and Co., Ltd., 1968.

Footpaths Committee. *Report of the Footpath Committee.* London: Her Majesty's Stationery Office, 1968.

Forestry Commission. *Public Recreation in National Forests: A Factual Study.* London: Her Majesty's Stationery Office, 1968.

Gardner, J. F. *Right of Ways.* London: Oyez Publications, No. 55, 1965.

Griffin, James D. "Land Use Planning: New Mexico's Green Belt Law." *National Resources Journal* 8 (1968): 190–97.

Haar, Charles M., ed. *Law and Land: Anglo-American Planning Practice.* Cambridge: Harvard University Press and M.I.T. Press, 1964.

Harris, Bryan. *An Outline of the Law Relating to Common Land and Public Access to the Countryside.* London: Sweet and Maxwell, Ltd., 1965.

Herring, Francis W., ed. *Open Space and the Law.* Berkeley: Institute of Governmental Studies, University of California, 1965.

Hobhouse Committee. *Report of the National Park Committee.* Cmd. 7121. London: His Majesty's Stationery Office, 1947.

Jellis, Rosemary, ed. *Land and People: The Countryside for Use and Leisure.* London: British Broadcasting Corporation Publications, 1966.

Joint Committee on Open Space Land, Preliminary Report, John T. Knox, Committee Chairman, California Legislative. Sacramento; California Office of State Printing, 1969.

Labour Government. *The Land Commission.* Cmd. 2771. London: Her Majesty's Stationery Office, 1965.

————. *Leisure in the Countryside.* Cmd. 2928. London: Her Majesty's Stationery Office, 1966.

————. *Town and Country Planning.* Cmd. 3333. London: Her Majesty's Stationery Office, 1967.

Lake District Park Planning Board. *Report of Traffic in the Lake District.* London: National Parks Commission, 1965.

McHarg, Ian C. *Design with Nature.* Garden City, New York: Natural History Press, 1969.

Mandelker, Daniel. *Green Belts and Urban Growth: English Town and Country Planning in Action.* Madison: University of Wisconsin Press, 1962.

Marlowe, A. R. "The Law of Town and Country Planning." *The Listener.* January 28, 1965.

Martin, Anne. *Economics and Agriculture.* London: George Allen and Unwin, Ltd., 1958.

Matuszeski, William. "Less than Fee Acquisition for Open Space: Its Effects on Land Values." Philadelphia: Institute of Legal Research, University of Pennsylvania, 1966. Unpublished paper.

Miles, Roger. *Forestry and the English Countryside.* London: Faber and Faber, Ltd., 1967.

Montague, Lord. *The Gilt and the Gingerbread, Or How to Live in a Stately Home and Make Money.* London: Michael Joseph, 1967.

National Parks Commission (a). *The Coasts of Southwest England.* London: Her Majesty's Stationery Office, 1966.

———— (b), *The Coasts of Kent and Sussex.* London: Her Majesty's Stationery Office, 1966.

———— (c). *The Coasts of the Northwest.* London: Her Majesty's Stationery Office, 1966.

————(d). *Nineteenth Report of the National Parks Commission and First Report of the Countryside Commission.* London: Her Majesty's Stationery Office, 1968.

National Trust. *The National Trust Report, 1967–68.* National Trust, 42 Queen Anne's Gate, London, SW 1.

New Forest Committee. *Report of the New Forest Committee.* Cmd. 7245. London: His Majesty's Stationery Office, 1944.

Parliamentary Debates, House of Commons, 5th Series, 1966.

Peak Park Planning Board. *Building in the Peak.* Bakewell, Derbyshire, 1964.

————. *Peak District National Park Development Plan.* Bakewell, Derbyshire, 1955.

————. *Peak District National Park Development Plan, First Review.* Bakewell, Derbyshire, 1966.

————. *16th Annual Report of the Peak Park Planning Board, 1967–68.* Bakewell, Derbyshire, 1968.

Polanyi, Karl. *The Great Transformation.* New York: Farrar and Rinehart, Inc., 1944.

Potter, David M. *People of Plenty.* Chicago: University of Chicago Press, 1954.

Registrar General. *Review of England and Wales for the Year 1966 Part II: Population Tables.* London: Her Majesty's Stationery Office, 1968.

Roberts, E. F. "The Right to a Decent Environment: Progress along a Constitutional Avenue." In Malcolm Baldwin and James K. Page, Jr., eds. *Law and the Environment.* New York: Walker and Co., 1970.

Scott Committee. *Report of the Committee on Land Utilization in Rural Areas.* Cmd. 6378. London: His Majesty's Stationery Office, 1942.

Smith, Adam. *An Inquiry into the Nature and Causes of the Wealth of Nations.* Book III. New York: P. F. Collier and Son, 1909.

Stamp, L. Dudley. *Man and the Land.* London: Collins Clear-Type Press, 1964.

Strong, Ann Louise. *Open Spaces for Urban America.* Prepared for the U.S. Department of Housing and Urban Development. Washington, D. C.: U.S. Government Printing Office, 1965.

Sutherland, Douglas. *The Landowners.* London: Anthony Blond, Ltd., 1968.

Swisher, Carl Brent. *The Supreme Court in Its Modern Role.* New York: New York University Press, 1958. Quote on pp. 179–80 reprinted by permission of New York University Press.

Tansley, A. G. *Britain's Green Mantle.* London: George Allen and Unwin, Ltd., 1965.

Tate, W. E. *The English Village Community and the Enclosure Movement.* London: Victor Gollancz, Ltd., 1967.

Trent River Authority. *Water Resources—A Preliminary Study.* Trent River Authority, 206 Derby Road, Nottingham, England, 1968.

Uthwait Committee. *Report of the Expert Committee on Compensation and Betterment.* Cmd. 6386. London: His Majesty's Stationery Office, 1942.

Weller, John. *Modern Agricultural and Rural Planning.* London: The Architectural Press, 1968.

Wenkam, Robert, "Hawaii's Statewide Land-Use Zoning: A First of the Nation." *Cry California,* Winter 1967–68, pp. 32–38.

Wordsworth, William. *Guide to the Lakes.* 5th Ed., London: Henry Frowds, 1906.

INDEX